T0194595

PREVIOUS BOOKS

Spiritual Wisdom for Peace on Earth From Sananda
Channeled through David J Adams

LOVE is the **KEY.** Part 1
Spiritual Wisdom from Germain
Channeled through David J Adams

LOVE is the **KEY.** Part 2
Spiritual Wisdom from Germain
Channeled through David J Adams

WE ARE ALL ONE
Spiritual Wisdom from The Masters of Shambhala
Channeled through David J Adams

ENLIGHTENMENT AND ILLUMINATION
Spiritual Wisdom from Djwahl Khul
Channeled through David J Adams

COSMIC SYMPHONY OF LOVE

SPIRITUAL WISDOM FROM
HILARION

CHANNELED THROUGH
DAVID J ADAMS

authorHOUSE®

AuthorHouse™
1663 Liberty Drive
Bloomington, IN 47403
www.authorhouse.com
Phone: 1 (800) 839-8640

© 2019 David J Adams. All rights reserved.

No part of this book may be reproduced, stored in a retrieval system, or transmitted by any means without the written permission of the author.

Published by AuthorHouse 08/09/2019

ISBN: 978-1-7283-2288-9 (sc)
ISBN: 978-1-7283-2286-5 (hc)
ISBN: 978-1-7283-2287-2 (e)

Library of Congress Control Number: 2019911663

Print information available on the last page.

Any people depicted in stock imagery provided by Getty Images are models, and such images are being used for illustrative purposes only. Certain stock imagery © Getty Images.

The Front Cover Sacred Geometry is called the 'Labyrinth of Divine Peace'. The Labyrinth was painted and photographed by Kaye Ogilvie, Intuitive artist from Queensland, Australia and based on a concept channeled through David J Adams. The Labyrinth was walked at the Marine Meditations in 2009 and 2010.

Back cover Photo was taken on the camera of David J Adams, the T shirt was created by Tie Dye artist, Ruth Cary Cooper from USA.

This book is printed on acid-free paper.

Because of the dynamic nature of the Internet, any web addresses or links contained in this book may have changed since publication and may no longer be valid. The views expressed in this work are solely those of the author and do not necessarily reflect the views of the publisher, and the publisher hereby disclaims any responsibility for them.

DEDICATION

I Dedicate this book to my children, Nicky and Suzi, my grandchildren, Lauren, Matthew and Emily, and my great grandchildren, Ruby–Rae and Peyton, for they and others of the next generations will carry the Light forward and create the Peace that we all yearn for.

ABOUT THE AUTHOR

ADAMS, David John Patrick

Born: 28th April 1943

At: Mountain Ash, Glamorgan, South Wales, UK.

Moved to South Australia in 1971, Currently living in the southern suburbs of the city of Adelaide.

Began his Spiritual Journey as a result of the Harmonic Convergence in late 1987.

In 1991, he was asked by Beloved Master Germain to undertake a global Meditation based on, and working with, the Consciousness of the Oceans, which was called the Marine Meditation.

In 2009 he was asked to address a Peace Conference in Istanbul to speak of the Marine Meditation and his work for World Peace through meditation.

He is a Songwriter, a Musician, an Author and Channel, but most of all a **SERVANT OF PEACE**.

David began bringing through information from a variety of Masters and Cosmic Beings in the form of Meditations around 1991. It was not, however, until after the year 2000 that he began to channel messages in group situations and in individual sessions. Most of these messages were not recorded or transcribed so remain shared with only a few people, but in 2009 the messages being brought through in the weekly Pendragon Meditation group began to be recorded and transcribed by Kath Smith and sent out around the world on David's own Pendragon network.

David's special Guide and Mentor has been 'The Germain, the I am that I am', but he has also worked extensively with – and channeled - Sananda, Hilarion, Djwahl Khul, AA Michael, The Merlin, The Masters of Shambhala, as well as Arcturian Sound Master Tarak and his own Home Trinity Cosmic Brother Ar'Ak.

(Contact email – <u>djpadams8@tpg.com.au</u>)

ACKNOWLEDGEMENTS

I, David J Adams, would like to acknowledge three special Earth Angels.

Heather Niland/Shekina Shar - who helped me to awaken to my Journey in 1987 and connected me to my Beloved Friend "The Germain", she was a mentor, guide and teacher way ahead of her time.

Meredith Pope – who walked in the same shoes as me in those difficult early years as a fellow 'weekender' at The EarthMother Centre, and was - and still is - an inspiration to me.

Krista Sonnen – An Harmonic and Earthwalker, who helped to build the bridges to my Spiritual and Cosmic friends by persistently urging me to allow them to speak through me in private sessions, then in group sessions. Without her support these messages would not be here.

I would further like to acknowledge **Kath Smith** – A spiritual Being of immense Love and Joy who initiated the recording and transcribing of the messages received in Pendragon so that the messages from our 'other Dimensional friends' would not be lost forever. Also **Takara Shelor,** who combined her Global Water Dolphin Meditation with the Marine Meditation in 1998 and has organized the Marine Meditation website as an adjunct to her own Dolphin Empowerment website ever since. Also **Kaye Ogilvie**, Intuitive Spiritual Artist, who Painted all the Labyrinths walked during the Marine Meditations, as well as many other inspirational images that have assisted my Journey of Growth.

I also acknowledge all those here in Australia and those throughout the World who have supported me and encouraged me over the years, and in particular, **Barbara Wolf and Margaret Anderson**, who's vision and hard work has made this book possible.

BLESSINGS OF LOVE, JOY AND PEACE TO EACH AND EVERY ONE OF YOU.

DAVID J ADAMS

FOREWORD

We Humans live in the concept of "Linear Time', which divides 'Time' into minutes, hours, days, months, etc. and goes in a straight line from 'Past' through 'Present' to 'Future', consequently we give importance to the date on which something happens. Our Spiritual and Cosmic Friends are not bound by such constraints, they operate in the **'Now'** moment, so although the messages within this book have 'dates' attached to them, they are, essentially, **TIMELESS**.

Some messages do, of course, refer to specific events, such as the Equinox or the Solstice, or even some man made event, however, the underlying message is always **TIMELESS**. So we ask, when you read these messages, that you accept them as having importance within the **'Now Moment'** of your lives. Although we have given the date of receipt at the end of each message, they are not in sequential 'linear time' order.

All messages were received within the Pendragon Meditation Circle and always began with the 'Sounding" of the Tibetan Bowls, the Blessings Chimes, the Drum, and occasionally other percussion instruments. Many of the messages make reference to these Sound frequencies.

Let the messages speak to your Heart, for that is what they were intended to do when they were given by **Master Hilarion**.

Blessings of Love, Peace and Joy

David J Adams

INTRODUCTION

Hilarion began working with me in 1999 when he and Djwahl Khul formed a Trinity of Masters with Beloved Germain to continue to work on the Global Marine Meditation that Beloved Germain had instigated with me in 1991. The Meditation designed to connect Humanity with the Consciousness of the Oceans and all the Beings of Light within the Oceans. From time to time he would come through me as an individual Master and gift Humanity with words of Wisdom, as well as working with me as part of the Council voice of the Masters of Shambhala.

Many of his words of Wisdom were lost to Humanity – as were words of Wisdom from other Masters and Cosmic Ambassadors - as they were never recorded and transcribed in the early years. Thanks to the efforts of Kath Smith when she joined the Meditation group in 2008, more recent words of

Wisdom have been preserved and are presented here in this book.

His words have always sought to uplift and guide us towards a greater understanding of ourselves in our search for Enlightenment and Illumination, our personal responsibilities and our Community and Global responsibilities.

I hope you will find within the words of his messages in this book an upliftment of Spirit and an enhancement of the Light that **already exists within each one of you.**

Blessings of Love, Peace and Joy.

David J Adams
(djpadams8@tpg.com.au)

CONTENTS

Dedication v
About the Author.. vii
Acknowledgements ix
Foreword xi
Introduction.. xiii

1   All Sacred Geometry is a Melody of Light 1
2   You are the Light for the Rest of Humanity 9
3   Cosmic Symphony of Love 13
4   Healing in Oneness 17
5   Sea of Love..25
6   Your Heart Does Not Sit in Judgement
    of Others,..30
7   Reclaiming the Unity of Your Soul.................. 34
8   You are Never the Victim of
    Circumstances 39
9   Freedom is the Acceptance of All as
    Equal 44
10 Personal Responsibility 49

11 'Heart of Oneness' 54

12 'Newborns' 57

13 Shambhala of Earth Mother's Heart 63

14 No One Enslaves You Any More 67

15 Helping to Build a Heaven on Earth 73

16 We are in Awe of the Illumination
    Radiating Forth from the Earth Planet 79

17 Enabling Others to Find the Light
    Within Themselves 85

18 You are All Human Rainbows 91

19 Breathe 94

20 Your Heart is the Receptor of Light and
    Sound...98

21 We are All Energy Beings in Different
    Forms.. 103

22 Sound the Blessings Chimes 108

23 The Mind is the Foundation on Which
    We Build the Mansion of our Heart 113

24 Embrace the 'Source' of All Light 120

25 Your Inner Sun of Divine Love 124

26 Much is Happening Beneath the Surface 128

27 Love and Joy and Peace Exist
    Everywhere 134

28 Allow Yourselves to Grow, and Allow
    Others to Grow 139

29 We Empower Each Other with our
    Sharing 143

Glossary 151
Songlines – Names and Approximate Routes 155
How to Make Your own Blessings Chimes 159

1

ALL SACRED GEOMETRY IS A MELODY OF LIGHT

(The circle begins with the Sound of the Tibetan Bowl, the Blessings Chimes and the drum)

Greetings, Dear Hearts, I am Hilarion.

It may seem at times that messages are getting very repetitive, it is like a record going around and around and playing only one phrase. It is important that this happens because Humans have a very short attention span, and for your Spiritual Friends to get a message through to you that you understand and absorb, it needs to be repeated.

Therefore this idea of Love, Joy and Harmony is coming through time and time again. In the Jesus message of a few weeks ago, it was indicated that this is your natural state, but you have forgotten this. You tend to think that your natural state is to be in pain and hurt and to be depressed, but the reality is that you were born to be Loving, you were born to be Joyful, you were born to be in Harmony.

What your friends are saying to you now is that it is time for you to once again embrace what you have always had! It is not something new, it is something that you began your life with.

When you look at babies when they come into the World first of all, literally they are looking out into nothingness, and they are Joyful, because they are communicating, and they are seeing, in different Dimensional Frequencies than adults are. Your Spirit friends are saying to you that you can be like that once again, you can be totally at ease with other Dimensional Frequencies. You can be in Love, be in Harmony, be in Joy, ***if you choose to be!***

If you are going to move into a new Earth Dimensional Frequency, what is it that you want to take into that frequency? do you want to take your depressions with you? do you want to take your pain with you? do you want to take your hurts with you? or do you want to move into a new Dimension and take your

Joy, your Love and your Harmony with you? if it is the latter, then you need to start to focus on those things now!

This is what the messages have been about!, this is what the Meditations have been about! working within your Hearts, not to *create* these energies - because they already exist - but to *reactivate* the energies that you brought to the Earth at the beginning of your existence, not only at the beginning of this reincarnation, but when you *first* came to this Earth.

You came with a purpose, and that purpose was to **Create a World of Light, a World of Love, of Joy, and of Harmony,** It is time to start remembering that! It is time to start reactivating what is at the core of your Being. It is time for you to switch channels in your life, to stop focusing on that channel which draws the Light down, and instead switch to the channel which elevates the Light into your lives, that you can become that Light.

So once again focus on the Heart, because it begins with the Heart. Focus purely and simply on that aspect of your Heart Chakra that *IS* your Love, your Joy, your Harmony, your Pure Light. You may have to dig through the debris of this lifetime in order to

3

find those little sparks of Light – but they are there. It is time to go into your Heart and find them.

This one (*David*) said this to the Gathering in Istanbul recently, ***"Walk into your Heart and look for Divine Peace, you will find it because Divine Peace is a natural state of Being"***. What is unnatural is the state that you have allowed yourselves to become, So it is time for choosing – right from this moment it is time to choose. If you move into your Heart and you choose to embrace the Light, the Love, the Peace, the Harmony, ***that*** will begin to infuse your whole body. It is a constant matter of choice, every moment of every day it is about choosing.

Everything that happens in your lives, everything you see, everything you feel, everything you touch, presents you with the opportunity to choose the way you react. The more frequently you react with Love, with Joy, with Harmony and with Light, the more you create a World which reflects that. I think that is the kind of World that we all desire to have. We all desire to be in a space of Love, a space of Joy, a space of Happiness. It comes from inside the Heart and radiates outwards.

You impact on others in ways you do not yet understand, but you do not need to understand, because you are not trying to convert others to your way of thinking, you are simply showing others your way of ***Being***. It is an important difference. Show them your way of ***Being***, that is what Ascension for each individual Being is all about. It is about having the courage, finally, to return to where you were at the beginning. To embrace the Light within yourself so totally that you ***become that Light*** in your relationships with others.

You will be challenged every step of the way, because the energies of 'control' are still very firmly in existence within this World. So every moment of every day you will face the challenge, you will face the choice of how you will react to what is happening around you.

Move into your Heart, make your choice from the Light within your Heart. The more you do that, the easier it becomes to make that choice.

As was indicated previously, at the upcoming Solstice the Earth will be 'nudged' into a new Dimensional Frequency that has been prepared by the ***'Harmonics'***. There will not be major disruptions because the work has already been done to balance and Harmonize the Earth into its new Frequencies. It will provide each and every person with an opportunity to make a dramatic change to their perceptions of themselves, and their perceptions of life itself. You don't have to wait for the Solstice, you can begin to make those choices now within your Hearts – to choose Light, to choose Peace, to choose Love, to choose Harmony.

If you are faced with a challenge and you don't initially make the choice of moving into Love and Light, ***don't beat yourself up***, you are recognizing the choice you have made, so honour that choice, then step back and choose again, because you understand that you ***DO*** have choice.

Take a moment to just imagine that you are wandering around inside your Heart Chakra, looking at all the beautiful walls you have surrounded yourself with, and begin to notice the decorations on those walls, the Sacred Geometry that covers each and every wall of your Heart Chakra. Begin to understand that Sacred Geometry is simply your reminder of the Light, the Love, the Joy and the Harmony that is at the core of your Being.

Feel free to walk up to any wall and look more closely at the Sacred Geometric patterns, the hieroglyphs of your past. You will not find any shadows or any darkness upon those walls - *there is only Light* – Allow yourself to understand what is written on the walls of your Heart Chakra, it is your private message from your *Soul Self*, your diary, if you like, of all your past existences from the very beginning of time.

Give yourself permission to absorb the energy of all that is written, and to feel the power of your own Being reflecting back to you by what has been written. Move closer to the walls and *Listen*, and you will hear the Melodies of Light, for all Sacred Geometry is a Melody of Light, one that resonates with every aspect of your Being. Listen to that inner voice of your Heart, and it will sing to you songs of great Joy, of great Love, of great Harmony, and within those songs you will find your *Source* – *THE ENERGY OF INFINITY.*

You may have walked around Churches and Cathedrals and Mosques and Temples and wondered, and looked with Awe at the magnificence of the designs on the walls and ceilings, well, Dear Hearts, You have such wondrous designs on the walls of your own Heart Chakra – *A record of all that has ever been within you.*

There is no judgement within your Heart, there is only allowance of what has been, and what is meant to be. Everything is an invitation to *BE* – to *BE* the Light that you have always been, to *BE* the Light that you have brought to this Planet - to assist this Planet.

ALLOW IT TO BE!

Blessings, I am Hilarion.

(7th December 2009)

2

YOU ARE THE LIGHT FOR
THE REST OF HUMANITY

(The Circle opens with the Sounds of the Tibetan Bowls and the Blessings Chimes)

Greetings, Dear Hearts, I am Hilarion.

See yourselves drawing in through your crown chakra a beautiful Golden Light, allowing it to flow down through your body, connecting, activating, embracing each and every chakra within your body, progressively filling yourself with this Golden Light. Know with the greatest of certainty that this Gold Light is flowing through you from your own Higher Self. Your own Higher Self connecting, filtering, then amplifying the Gold Light of the Great Central Sun, cascading down into your Being, into each and every chakra, and each and every cell of your

9

body, into each and every Light Particle of your Multidimensional Being.

The Gold Light agitates and activates every particle of your Being, feel yourself becoming this beautiful Gold Light. As you breathe, breathe in the Gold Light, breathe out the Gold Light, fill the whole area surrounding your Being with Gold Light energy.

The Gold Light is the Light of Initiation, this Gold Light is initiating you into a greater connection with your Higher Self, drawing you closer and closer, becoming *ONE* with your Higher Self, allowing your mind and your brain to integrate with the visions of your Higher Self, with the perspective of your Higher Self. Lifting your Consciousness in this Dimension to connect with your Higher Self, to see your Light with a new, clearer, more powerful, perspective, allowing your mind and your brain to work more closely with your Higher Self, to let go of resistance to that which is beyond your mind's current comprehension.

Allow the visions of your Higher Self to become a part of your mind and your brain, open to that which is beyond your physical vision, your physical understanding. Through this connection of Gold

Light, you will move with ease and grace through all the changes that are taking place on your Planet at this time.

Feel the power of your own Divine Self, feel the upliftment of Spirit within you. Embrace the Gold Light, focus on the Gold Light, feel your inner Vision becoming clearer and clearer as you allow more of the Higher Vision of your Soul to become part of your daily reality.

Look upon your Planet through the eyes of your Higher Self, through the Rays of Gold Light, embrace it, become totally open to the flow of this energy.

You have come here at this time to be a Light for the rest of Humanity. Embrace that within your Heart and your mind and your Total Being. You Light the way for others, you do not command others along that path, you simply *are* the ***Light*** that Lights the Planet.

Feel yourself begin to move forward into the future of Peace, Love, Joy and Harmony that you agreed to create upon this Planet.

We are all with you, we are all a part of the process of Enlightenment. Feel the Gold Light within you now harmonizing every aspect of your Being, improving your Vision and your sight.

Within the Gold Light you are a part of **all that is**, free flowing, embracing. Draw in from the Cosmos at this time the Rays of all the Masters, all the colours of the Rainbow. Bring them into your Gold Light.

The integration of your individual Human Consciousness with your individual Higher Self is paramount at this time, to allow your own Human Consciousness to see beyond the limitations of the Dimension in which you reside.

Work with the Gold Light to assist this integration, and allow yourselves to see what is beyond this Dimension.

I am Hilarion, I bless you.

And so it is.

(2nd August 2010)

3

COSMIC SYMPHONY OF LOVE

(The circle opens with the Sounds of the Tibetan bowls, the rattle and the Blessings Chimes)

Open your Hearts and call in to your Being the *'Cosmic Symphony of Love'* that has been gifted to the Earth Planet at the time of the Equinox. Feel it resonate in every aspect of your Being, creating within you a new frequency of Sound, lifting the rhythm of your Heart beat to the new resonance of the Earth Planet itself.

This is a time when the Earth itself has been raised in vibrational frequency and it is now up to each individual upon the Earth to choose to move into this new resonance of Sound or to remain in the darkness and duality of the past.

Greetings, Dear Hearts, I am Hilarion.

I remind you, Dear Hearts, that you continue to exist on a Planet of **'free will'**. Whatever is gifted to the Earth from the Cosmos remains a choice for each of you to make. Nothing that is gifted to you from the Cosmos is forced upon you, it is simply offered with the deepest of Love.

Of course, Dear Hearts, all of us who are assisting you in other Dimensional Frequencies are hoping that each one of you grasps these opportunities and lifts yourselves into the New Dimensional Frequency of the Earth, for as each Being of Light lifts into this New Dimensional Frequency it stabilises the Earth in that new frequency.

We are delighted to know that you share the gifts we offer with so many others around the Earth, giving them also the opportunity to choose the Divine Love, to choose the New Vibrational Frequencies of Sound, to choose to Ascend with Beloved Earth.

Make no judgment of those who do not choose immediately, for each of you is on your own journey, on your own pathway, and each of you will be awakened at a different time, at a time that is right for you.

We ask you to continue sharing your Love, your Light, your wisdom, your knowledge and your Love with all those you meet and all those you know, for Love spreads quickly and the Earth embraces each Being who offers themselves in service to the Earth.

The Equinox was most powerful, the *'Symphony of Love'* that was gifted to the Earth is resonating throughout the Crystalline structure of the Earth, and through all the Songlines of the Earth, and if you choose to embrace it, it will uplift you into the *Dimension of Ecstasy.*

When you come together in Circle, in Council, you amplify the Love within your Hearts and you enlighten more and more of the Earth Planet simply by breathing your Love out across the Earth.

You may not yet be aware of the power of the Circle, not only this Circle, but many other Circles around the Earth that come together to share, to embrace, to *BE* the Light of the Earth.

You continue, of course, to exist within your linear time and therefore it may seem that things move slowly, but from where we sit, Dear Hearts, the changes upon your Earth and within your Earth and within all upon your Earth are moving at an incredible pace.

You will soon become aware of some of these changes that are taking place across your Earth Planet in the Hearts of Humanity. More and more Light is being generated and being spread across the Earth and the darkness of the past is fading rapidly.

Your assistance is always required, not so much in what you do, but in the way you are, the Light you are, the Joy you are.

Take time each day to BE in the stillness of your Heart and allow the glow of Joy to shine forth and embrace all those around you.

(29th September 2014)

4

HEALING IN ONENESS

(The Gathering opens with the Sounds of the Tibetan Bowl, the Drum and the Peace and Harmony Chimes)

Allow the Sound Vibrations to permeate your whole body, relaxing every part of yourself, clearing everything from your minds except the Oneness of all that is.

Greetings, Dear Hearts, I am Hilarion

It has been some considerable time since I was last within your Sacred Space, and I am delighted to be here now, for I wish to speak to you about another aspect of Oneness. Hopefully to enable you to come to a greater understanding of yourself, of your Planet

and of Oneness, and this has to do very much with
Healing.

Dear Hearts, you have been accustomed during your
lifetime, indeed, during your many lifetimes, of
perceiving everyone as being separate from yourself,
consequently when you have worked with healing
energies you have always directed those energies,
sent those energies, outside yourself, reaching
out to others, perhaps in a healing room situation,
perhaps healing at a distance, sending out your
healing energies, **This**, Dear Hearts, is accepting
and acknowledging the perception of separation,
of duality. It is now time to begin to embrace the
reality of Oneness, and to perceive all other people
as being a part of you, and if, Dear Hearts, if they
are a part of you, you do not need to direct your
energies, to send your energies elsewhere.

Because your minds, Dear Hearts, are constructed
to enable you to exist within your Dimension of
duality, it is very difficult for it to comprehend that
there is no separation, You are One, so today I am
here to invite you to change your thinking, to change
your attitude about Healing, and indeed, about the
World that you live in.

Some years ago, Dear Hearts, through this one (*David*), we said to you that the Oceans of your World do not separate land masses, they join land masses, and when you place Healing energy, Loving energy, into the Ocean in one place, that flows through the Oceans to all the land masses and all of Humanity all around the World.

You see, Dear Hearts, this is the Oneness, everything is One, you are not separated, not by Oceans, not by time - time as you see it, your linear time – so, Dear Hearts, think of your friends, think of strangers around the World as being a part of you. *They are a part of the Ocean of Love within your Heart.* Let that sink into you for a moment, Dear Hearts, there is nothing and no one outside of yourself - they are all existing within the Ocean of Love within your Heart.

Now, if you embrace that, Dear Hearts, you suddenly realize that sending energy anywhere is an illusion and totally unnecessary. You often use the term 'Distance Healing' which immediately recognizes or establishes, if you like, that the subject of your healing is outside yourself. I am asking you, Dear Hearts, to now begin to think and feel that they are instead *'within'* yourself, so when you are aware that someone is sick and in need of healing energies, draw their names into your Heart and bathe them in your energies of Healing Love. By so doing, Dear Hearts, you are embracing them as part of the **Oneness of You**.

You will find, no doubt, that this brings up a conflict within yourself, for so long you have been steeped in this concept of others being separate from yourselves, but you are moving from the Dimension of Separation into the Dimension of Oneness and you need to reflect this change by doing things, thinking things, believing things differently. You cannot talk of Oneness and then practice Separation simply because separation is always the way you have done things! So, Dear Hearts, you need to begin **doing** things within the Dimension of **Oneness.**

You may have noticed in a number of messages recently we have spoken to you about a 'change of attitude', and this is another aspect of that - **changing your attitude, changes your actions.**

Events happen on your Earth Planet that appear to be distant from you, it may be a natural catastrophe or a man made horrific event, and you are immediately moved to send your Love to that particular part of your World, ***do not do that anymore!*** instead, Dear Hearts, embrace that event within your Heart as part of your Oneness, and bathe it in healing Love, the healing Love that exists deep within your Heart, you are then acknowledging and accepting everything that happens upon your Earth Planet as part of the ***Oneness that you are***. It is no longer something that is happening in some distant part of your World, it is something that is happening deep within *you*.

You see, Dear Hearts, the problem with working from an attitude of separation is that you disconnect yourself. When you disconnect yourself you open yourself to judgement, blame, anger, all these things. As we have said, Dear Hearts, you may not always like what you see, but that is a judgement of separation, and you cannot resolve things by separating yourself from them, You need to be within the Oneness in order to change the happenings on the Earth Planet.

You may sit with someone who is ill, and you may see yourself reaching out to them, giving them, sending them your energy. I am here to give you an alternative - embrace them, bring them within your Heart, No, no, no, not even bring them within your Heart, Dear Ones, acknowledge that they ***ARE*** a part of your Heart, That is the Oneness, and when you accept that they are part of your Heart, you begin to heal yourself and because they are part of yourself, you begin to heal them.

This may sound quite radical to your minds, so steeped are they in separation, but I ask you to think of it, Dear Hearts, just as we asked you to think many years ago of the Oceans of your World as joining you rather than separating you, we are now asking you to think of others, to think of your Planet, not as separate from you, but as Part of you, part of the Oneness of all that is.

Oneness is not a concept that we are asking you to embrace, Dear Hearts, it is the ***Truth of reality, You are all One.*** and you have chosen to discover and embrace this Oneness by allowing yourselves to be in a foreign Dimension of Separation and Duality. This does represent a change of attitude within you, and it happens one step at a time, We know this, Dear Hearts, you know this, and so I come to you today and I ask you now to move within your Hearts and to begin to take practical steps to embrace the Dimension of Oneness.

Healing is such an important part of your thought processes. When you change the way you think about healing you change the way you think about yourself, so I ask you now to think of someone you know who is in need of healing at this time, and instead of sending them your healing Love, speak their name aloud, bring them into your Heart, acknowledge that they *ARE* within your Heart and simply bathe them in the Light of Healing Love that exists within your Heart, and you will find, and they indeed will find, that this healing is much more powerful than anything you have experienced before, because you are healing within the Oneness of all that is. You are taking away the distance of separation, for in reality, Dear Hearts, there *is no distance*, that is an illusion, just as your linear time is an illusion, distance is an illusion, it is a creation of your Dimension of duality, your Dimension of separation.

Now, because, of course, you continue to exist in this fragmented Dimension of separation and duality your mind screams out 'how silly is that, distance does not exist?', but if you begin to understand that this is all *'Attitude'*, and if you change your attitude, you change everything, then perhaps – perhaps - Dear Hearts, you can begin to lift yourself into the Dimension of Oneness.

There is an old phrase that I know has been used for eons of time on your Planet, it's the phrase, 'The tyranny of distance'. Well, Dear Hearts, it is time to dispense with this tyranny of distance, you do that simply by acknowledging and accepting that you are all One, you all exist within the Oneness and therefore there is no distance, everything, everyone, every Being of Light upon your Earth Planet exists within your Heart, within your Consciousness, so healing needs to take place within your Heart.

Do not waste energy sending it anywhere, use your energy to embrace more tightly everything within the Oneness. and you will discover, Dear Hearts, that your healing energy is ***Profound.***

I thank you for accepting me within your Sacred Space today and I hope that I have given you some food for thought, Dear Hearts, I embrace you within my own Heart, for we are all One.

(27th November 2017)

5

SEA OF LOVE

(The Circle opens with the Sounds of the Tibetan Bowls, the Blessings Chimes, and the Drum)

Feel the energies of Love flowing from deep within your Heart out into the World and out into the Cosmos, sharing the unique aspect of yourself as a part of the Oneness of all that is. Allow your energies to become limitless. Let go of every strand of separateness that remains within your Being and allow yourself to feel fully and completely a part of the Whole.

Feel the expansion within you, experience floating in a *'Sea of Love'* that *IS* the essence of Oneness. It may feel a little strange at first to simply allow yourself to float in this *Sea of Love*, connecting with everything and everyone.

This is the next step of your journey, Dear Ones, coming to terms with letting go of your separateness and embracing the wholeness, and allowing yourself to experience life on the Earth Planet through the energy of wholeness from within the *Sea of Love*.

Greetings, Dear Hearts, I am Hilarion.

The energies of the Earth have changed so dramatically over recent times that coming to be with you is so different now, there is such an energy of Oneness growing through and upon the Earth that we do not have to lower our vibrational frequencies to the extent we did before.

Can you feel my energies, Dear Hearts, vibrating as part of yourself? Feel the upliftment within your Hearts, it is an amazing feeling, a feeling which we - your spiritual friends - exist in most of the time, a *'Sea of Love'*, and each one of you is a part now of that *Sea of Love*.

Look around you, Dear Hearts, see your connection with Earth Mother and your connection with the Cosmos and notice, Dear Hearts, there is no dividing line anymore, there is no separation anymore, there is only the Oneness of Love, and it is within this

Oneness of Love that you and the Earth Planet sit together and will grow in Consciousness, will awaken in the Light and the Love, and perceive everything totally differently.

This may, Dear Hearts, only occur for a brief period of time as you focus upon it here in this Circle, but know that as you are a part of this *Sea of Love* you can experience it at any time and you can share it at any time, not with your words, simply with your energies.

Expand, embrace - *BE* the Love of which you speak.

Your Spiritual friends will continue to assist you in every way possible, the Cosmos will continue to assist you in every way possible also, for this is an ongoing expansion into Oneness. You are experiencing the first taste of Oneness, and it tastes sweet does it not?

As you know, Dear Hearts, we endeavour to work with you at specific times of Cosmic alignment and we are coming up to the point of the Solstice once more. You may recall, Dear Hearts, at the last Solstice Earth Mother opened her Heart and shared the Magenta Light within her Heart, and that Light of Love is creating change upon the Earth as more and more Beings of Light awaken and come together in *'Oneness of purpose'*.

So at the upcoming Solstice there will be a new inflow of energy to the Earth Planet from deep at the centre of the Cosmos. The original *'Purple Ray'* that your good friend Germain has spoken of often is now being empowered into the Earth Planet to become One with the Magenta Light. The *Violet Flame* of *Divine Love* and *Divine Peace* will flow into the Earth Planet and move into the deepest areas of Earth Mother's Heart to come together with the *Magenta Light* and flow out into the World, to further change attitudes upon the Earth, bringing a greater and greater measure of balance and harmony, and more and more Beings of Light will be awakened by the new fusion of the Magenta Light and the Purple Ray.

Here tonight, Dear Hearts, feel that Purple Ray flowing into your Heart joining together with the Magenta Light within your Heart and expanding you even more, uplifting you even more as you float in the *Sea of Love*.

The veils of Light that have held you back are now evaporating, everything is becoming *One*, so I will ask you, Dear Hearts, at the time of the Solstice, to open yourself completely and invite into your Hearts the *Purple Ray* to join the *Magenta Light* and

FLOOD THE EARTH WITH THE 'SEA OF LOVE'.

(14th December 2015)

6

YOUR HEART DOES NOT SIT IN JUDGEMENT OF OTHERS,

(The circle opens with the Sounds of the Tibetan Bowls and the Drum)

Allow the Sounds of the bowls and the drum to reverberate deep within your Hearts, drawing forth the energies of Divine Love that are at the essence of your Heart, and allow those energies of Divine Love to flow through every aspect of your Being, filling your physical body, your energy body, your emotional body and your spiritual body with the pure energies of Divine Love.

And as you fill yourself with the energies of Divine Love, allow those energies to flow freely from you, to embrace all those within the Circle, to join together with the Divine Love of everyone within the Circle, to create a powerful vibration of Divine Love in the Oneness of all that is, and through your Hearts focus that Oneness energy of Divine Love upon the Earth Planet itself, surrounding it, permeating it, becoming one with the Earth Planet, that all may be the vibration of Divine Love.

Greetings Dear Hearts, I am Hilarion. I thank you for connecting your Love with the whole of the Earth Planet, allowing yourselves to become *'consciously'* a part of the Oneness of all that is, for it is together in this Oneness that you will begin to create the Earth of the future, an Earth that is not separate and divided, an Earth which lives and breathes in Unity and Oneness, where no individual Being is perceived as less than another, where all are accepted for the Light and the Love they bring to the whole.

The Light of each individual Being is important to the whole, is valued by the whole, and valuable to the whole. *Your Heart does not sit in judgement of others, it sits in Oneness with others,* so in the new Earth frequency it is important to focus on your Heart, and to embrace All as One.

We recognise that there is still difficulty for Humanity to let go of the judgements of the mind, and to fully embrace the Oneness of the Heart, but this will change progressively as time moves on, so be strong, Dear Hearts, be balanced each day within your Heart and make your choices in life from the Love within your Heart, and you will find the world around you will become more peaceful, more joyful.

It is time for ALL the *'way showers'* to come together within the energy of Divine Love, and to reach out to all those who need more Light and more Love and more understanding in their lives, and share with them the wisdom within your Hearts, the wisdom of Unity, the wisdom of Oneness.

Each moment, each day, when you first awaken, see the Earth Planet in your mind's eye as a baby being bathed by the Light of Love within your Hearts, and gift that baby - *your new Earth* - the full power of the *Divine Love* that you possess, knowing that as you do this you will be allowing the Earth Planet to grow into its own Oneness, maturing, becoming a source of Divine Love within itself.

Dear Hearts, the future of the Earth is yours to create, do so from the Love in your Hearts.

(29th July 2013)

7

RECLAIMING THE UNITY
OF YOUR SOUL

(The Circle opens with the Sounds of the Tibetan Bowls and the Blessings Chimes.)

Draw deep into the centre of your Being, the many individual frequencies of Light and Colour that are currently within this Circle, and embrace the Sound Vibrations of the Tibetan Bowls and the Blessings Chimes, enabling the energies of Love deep within your Heart to be uplifted into Joyfulness, into Bliss, and into Ecstasy, as you feel your whole Being becoming lighter and lighter, as you move your Consciousness from the physicality of the third Dimension into the higher frequencies of Light in the fourth and the fifth and even higher Dimensions, *reclaiming the Unity of your Soul and its connection with the Universe.*

Feel yourselves floating in a sea of Light and a sea of Sound, and breathe in the Oneness of the Universe, and feel yourself becoming an integral part of that Oneness.

Greetings, Dear Hearts, I am Hilarion,

I embrace you with the deepest Love within my Heart and welcome you to the Higher Dimensional Frequencies of Light, for when you are allowing yourselves to be in those Higher Dimensions of Light you are able to look down upon your Earth and see the panorama of your life - to see your life from beginning to end - for *everything is within the now.*

When you reside in your third dimensional body the veils are all around you, you cannot see beyond the moment, you cannot see beyond the day, but in your Higher Dimensional Soul Self you see everything, for you, Dear Hearts, have planned everything. *The script of your life has not been written by someone else, it has always been written by you.* It may well be, Dear Hearts, that in your third dimensional reality, situations have arisen that you did not create, but how you deal with those situations has always been YOUR choice, so you have always written the script of your life, and as you sit in your Higher Dimensional Soul-Self Frequency and look over your life, you do not become lost in the troughs, you see a progression, a pattern of existence that you have designed for your own learning, for your own Ascension, for the development of your own Consciousness.

More and more, Dear Hearts, you are being called by your own Soul-Self to move into the Higher Dimensional Frequencies, to see the pattern of your life as a whole, and to see and feel the joyfulness that this completed pattern exudes.

It is a bit like some of the wondrous creations that you have hanging on your wall at the moment, at the time that they were being made only small portions were obvious to the artist, it is not until they are completed and you step back and look at the wondrous nature of the completed item that you feel the true resonance of Joy within your Hearts - not only the artist, but all those who subsequently look upon the completed work of art - they also feel the Joy of the completed item.

The same happens with your lives, Dear Ones, you see only the mountain that is ahead of you, the valley below you, you do not hold your head up and see beyond the immediacy of what you face day in and day out, but when you accept the invitation of your Higher Soul-Self to move up in frequencies of Light and look at the whole pattern of *your personal work of art that is your life*, then - and only then - can you begin to feel the Joy building up inside you, radiating out from you, because you are looking at the Whole. Your perception and judgment of your life is different when you look at that life from a higher perspective, from the perspective of its wholeness, not its many individual components.

Dear Hearts, in your third Dimensional reality you ride the emotional waves, you perceive life in minutes and hours and days and months, and your emotions create your reality, for you cannot see the road ahead, but *in your Higher Soul-Self you see EVERYTHING, you SEE and you KNOW the meaning of your life.*

Most of you at this particular time are spending more and more of your time in your Higher Dimensional Soul Frequencies and you are seeing the true majesty of your life on Planet Earth - your many lives on Planet Earth - you see yourself in that '*coat of many colours'* that is spoken of in one of your religious documents.

You have always been Beings of a multitude of Colours, a multitude of Sound; you change and reflect according to those you have around you, but all of it, Dear Hearts, is written by you. Your lives have been a story book of searching for yourself, searching for Joy, and Bliss and Ecstasy, and you are now finding that Ecstasy in your Higher Dimensional Soul-Self.

Take time each day to sit in your Higher Soul- Self and express your gratitude for the wondrous work of art that YOU have created and called

'LIFE'

(2nd March 2015)

8

YOU ARE NEVER THE VICTIM
OF CIRCUMSTANCES

(The Circle opens with the Sounds of the Tibetan bowls and the Tingsha bells.)

Allow the vibrations of the bowls and the bells to lift you up into the embrace of your Soul Journey, feeling deep within your Being the Bliss and Joy of your new Soul Journey, a Soul Journey that enables you to look at the panorama of your existence on the Earth Planet at this time, giving you an overview of all that is happening around you, within you, and feel the Bliss of your Soul moving to fill every aspect of your physical Being, every aspect of your emotional Being, every aspect of your mental Being.

Embrace the Love that you are, and see yourself clearly as a Being of Love, a Being of Light, a Being of Bliss.

Greetings Dear Hearts, I am Hilarion.

It is with great pleasure that I embrace the beautiful energy of this Circle tonight, and feel the Love and the Bliss within each one of you, coming together to create a Oneness of Love, a Oneness of Bliss which radiates forth across the Planet touching every Being, assisting to open Hearts that are ready to birth their own energies of Bliss and Love.

This is truly a magical time upon the Earth Planet - and for Humanity as a whole - for this is a time of great change, and each and every one of you has done much work over recent times to prepare yourself for the shift into the new Dimensional frequencies - but nothing happens immediately! it takes time for each one of you to let go of old programmes, of old belief systems, and each of you will do it at a different pace than another. So never judge yourself against another, and never judge another against yourself. Simply embrace ALL with a deep feeling of Love.

This is the essence of your Soul Journey, a journey of acceptance, a journey of opening to the beauty and the power of Love within you, and as you embrace that power within you, you see the world around you begin to change in colour and complexion, for Love spreads quickly to fill the Hearts of many.

Dear Hearts, you are never the victim of circumstances, but you are always the product of your own choices!

That statement may seem a little provocative, for I can hear each and every one of you immediately react and say "but so many things have happened to me in my life, in my many lives, that have been created by others".

And on the surface, Dear Hearts, that is so, there are many times when 'things happen' in your life, but although you may not have initiated changes that take place in your life, you always have the choice of how you react to what happens in your life, and it is not the actual events that create your future. It is how YOU choose to react to those events that creates the reality of your life.

So think again upon that statement *"you are never victims, for you always have choice"*, and in the New Soul Dimension you choose to be Love, whatever happens or transpires around you in your life, you choose a Loving response, and as you choose the Loving response, you create a Loving environment.

So whatever the intentions of those who seek to create the change, *it matters not* once you accept that you choose the life you wish to create.

We accept, Dear Hearts, that this can at times be difficult, for you are in a world where relationships occur and become extremely important in your lives, but all relationships of meaning originate with a choice of Love - Loving Energies.

You can choose to feel hurt, you can choose to feel pain, you can choose to feel anger, or you can choose to embrace yourself with the energies of Love - and as you do that you create Joy, where on the surface previously, you felt there was no Joy.

In this New Dimension, the old ways are no more. The Soul Journey is about self-responsibility. It is about accepting that YOU choose in every moment of your life what you create.

You can acknowledge that another person has created a situation that you need to handle; but they, in creating that situation, cannot dictate your choices of how you react.

So it is time, as you face great changes upon your Planet and upon your relationships with others around you, it is time to accept and embrace personal responsibility for the choices you make.

So I repeat again *"You are never the victim of circumstances. You are only the product of the choices you make"*.

Dear Hearts I leave you with that statement, and ask that you allow it to sit within your Heart until you accept and acknowledge the truth of it.

(25th February 2013)

9

FREEDOM IS THE ACCEPTANCE OF ALL AS EQUAL

(The Circle opens with the Sounds of the Tibetan bowls and the Cosmic Tone)

Breathe in the connectedness of this Circle tonight, feeling the Oneness, feeling the Unity, and yet being totally aware of your individuality, your unique connection to all that is, for there is no whole without each and every one of you bringing your unique talents, your unique energies, your unique Light into the wholeness of the Universe, for you exist beyond the limitations of the Earth Planet. You are an integral part of the whole of the Universe.

Embrace and accept yourself as the magnificent Being of Light that you are. Do not limit your perception of yourself, for if you do, you automatically limit your perception of the magnificence of the whole.

Greetings Dear Hearts, I am Hilarion.

Many of your Earth years ago when Beloved Germain began to work with this one (*David*) on the Marine Meditation at the time of the Equinox, he always gave a theme for the year ahead, even before the advent of your Sacred Geometry Labyrinths, he always gave a theme, so I have come tonight to give you a theme for this year as you approach your Equinox, for although you are no longer participating necessarily in a Marine Meditation, it remains a time of great power, a time of coming together in Oneness, and therefore it is good to have a theme, to have a focus, and for this year of great change on your Planet I ask you to *"Focus upon Freedom".*

You may perceive yourself to be free, you are not incarcerated, you are not enslaved, but are you truly free? I ask you to think a moment on that, to think of what your understanding of freedom is, for although you may project it outwards and look at it in terms of being not in prison, or not Being a slave, *you may find that you are indeed enslaved or imprisoned*

by your own attitudes to life, by your own belief systems.

Freedom is the acceptance of ALL as EQUAL. You may have a belief system that puts you above others, a belief system that perceives differences rather than accepts uniqueness. As you move towards your Equinox I ask you take some time to examine your belief systems, your attitudes to yourself and to others upon this Planet, to other Beings of Light, to other Humans, to Animals, to Nature, to the whole of the Earth Planet itself.

Can you honestly say that you open your Heart in Love for all that is, without judgement, without condemnation? Dear Hearts, you are surrounded by the energies of fear. Do you take those fears into yourself and make judgements, or are you free, free in Love of all that is?

"Focus on freedom", redefine freedom in your life, in your perceptions, in your attitude. Are you enslaved by your circumstances in life, do you operate in life from Love or from a sense of duty? You see, Dear Hearts, 'duty' is an enslavement, **Love _is the true freedom_.** Are you free to speak your minds, to speak from your Hearts, or do you hold back lest you offend the sensibilities of others? You see, Dear Hearts, enslavement and incarceration is, in itself, an illusion. You perceive it in many different ways and you need to look at that in your lives, to understand what freedom really means for you.

So that, Dear Hearts, is my theme for your Marine Meditation deliberations for this year. *"Focus on Freedom"*, apply that to your Oceans, Dear Hearts, think of the creatures of the Oceans who are enslaved for your entertainment, and yet that is justified by many on the basis that if these creatures, these beautiful dolphins and whales were not there for your entertainment, you would have little concern for them in the wild, so you justify their enslavement by giving it noble motives.

What if all creatures were free, would you stop caring about them, would you stop caring about whales and dolphins if you did not see them behind bars, so to speak, if you are not entertained by them? Yes there are wonderful Beings of Light in the Oceans that are free, but some are not, and in your Hearts you know that while that situation continues on your Planet, *no one, NO ONE, accepts or knows freedom! for you only understand freedom when you understand yourselves.*

Meditation is always a time of going inside and discovering more about yourselves, and this will be the case at the time of your Equinox when you connect to others around the world.

Think, feel, and BE Freedom.

Blessings to all of you.

(3rd March 2014)

10

PERSONAL RESPONSIBILITY

(The Circle opens with the Sounds of the Tibetan Bowls and the Blessings Chimes)

Greetings, Beloveds, I am Hilarion. I come to speak to you tonight about personal responsibility.

You came to this Planet at the beginning of time as Beings of Light, for the purpose of creating a Planet of denseness, a Planet of duality, through which you would learn and grow, and ultimately return to the Light, and to the Heart of Source.

You have succeeded most admirably in creating such denseness and duality, and for eons of time you lost yourselves within that Dimension, and it is only of recent times that you have begun to swim to the surface of that denseness, and to begin to perceive, once more, the Light within yourself.

It is important to realise, Dear Ones, that everything upon your Planet is your creation, your personal and your collective creation.

Duality requires, of course, the creation of opposites, and you have created the opposite to Light.

Through those eons of time when you were lost in the density of your Planet, it became a matter of convenience to be able to apportion blame for all that is happening to that opposite you created. Evil - as opposed to good, dark - as opposed to Light, and it became so easy to apportion blame for all the problems that occurred within your Planet to the "dark forces".

You forgot that you created the illusion of darkness for purposes of your own growth.

In recent times we have spoken to you much about changing your perspectives, about letting go of the old paradigms, the old belief systems. Yet, in many instances you continue to focus upon the effects created by the "dark forces".

You are moving through this year of change, from duality into Oneness, from separation into Unity, and you cannot do that whilst continuing to blame others for what you perceive is going wrong in your world, or in your life.

It is time Dear Ones to accept personal responsibility for all that happens in your life.

If you focus within your Heart, purely on the Oneness of all that is, on the Unity, there is no room anymore for the "dark forces" to exist, for they were but a figment of your imagination in your duality, a necessity in order for you to learn.

Now it is time to let go of that illusion of opposites. Within Oneness there is no need for opposites in order to continue your learning.

Your learning now comes from within your Heart, from the Light you stored within your Heart at the beginning of time when you moved into the density, and created the opposites.

Embrace the Unity and the Oneness within your Heart. Do not perceive events that happen on your Planet that do not accord with your beliefs to be part of someone else, or something else.

Accept full responsibility for everything that is created on the Earth at this time.

Until you accept that personal responsibility, you cannot create the New Earth of Peace and Love, Joy and Harmony.

When we ask you to let go of those aspects of the past that no longer resonate for the New Earth, we speak also of what you have called in the past "the dark forces". They were, and are, an aspect of the illusion you created to learn your lessons.

It is time to let them go. It is time to focus purely on the Light within your Hearts. As you do, you multiply the Light quotient within the Earth Planet itself.

You begin to create true Oneness and Unity of purpose.

We, in other Dimensions, cannot command you to do these things. We can only draw them to your attention that you may choose whether you hold on to the past, or embrace the future, whether you continue to hold on to the "dark", or focus on the Light. ***The choice is yours***.

Personal freedom of choice you have always had on the Earth Planet. Now it is time to recognise that freedom of choice comes with responsibility.

Look into your Hearts. Ask yourself "what is it you wish to create in the New Earth?"

If you choose the Light, then let go of the "blame game", let go of "the dark", and feel the upliftment and the enlightenment within yourselves.

My blessings be upon you Dear Ones, and I thank you for sharing this with me tonight.

(30th January 2012)

11

'HEART OF ONENESS'

(The Circle opens with the Sounds of the Tibetan Bowls, the Blessings Chimes and the Drum)

Greetings, Dear Hearts, I am Hilarion

Feel the power of the Unity within this Circle, at this moment. Feel the Light move deep within your Hearts and feel your Hearts expand to form a Single Heart filled with Light, embracing each and every Heart within the Circle - coming into Oneness - and begin to awaken to the greater aspects of *Self*.

Through the Oneness of the Single Heart, embrace your multidimensional Being, feel yourself open wider and wider until there are no barriers, there are no limitations, you are One with all that is.

Within the 'Heart of Oneness' feel the immense power of Divine Love, feel your own contribution to this power of Divine Love, and again feel yourself open wider and wider. See the 'Heart of Oneness' become the Heart of the Earth Planet, and feel the immense power of the Divine Love of the Earth itself.

Feel the swirl of energies flowing through the Heart as it beats, pulsing Light out into the Universe and embracing Light from the Universe, becoming a part of the Universal flow of energy.

Feel yourself totally a part of the whole. Feel the beat of your Heart become the beat of the 'Heart of Oneness', and become the beat of the 'Heart of the Earth', and become the beat of the 'Heart of the Universe', and know with total certainty that Love is everything, that Light and dark are but the inflow and outflow of Love from the *'Heart of Oneness'*.

Know that each time your Heart beats, it sends out waves of Love, and those waves of Love will lift others upon the Planet up into a Higher Dimensional frequency of Light, of Joy, of Harmony.

Imagine if you will, the Earth as a single beating Heart filled with Love, pulsing, radiating that Love to all corners of the Universe, calling out to all ***"WE are One, in Light and in Love, WE are One"***, and as you imagine yourself within this Heart, there is no judgement of others, there is no comparisons with others, for you are all a part of the beat of this 'Heart of Oneness'.

Allow yourselves now to feel the upliftment of Joy as the 'Earth Heart' beats within you, and know that you will create through Love,

A world that is filled with Love,

A world that <u>breathes</u> Peace and Harmony,

A world that is filled with Joy.

Feel the pulsing of energy flowing through every fibre of your Being. Feel yourself uplifted.

We are all One.

We are all Love.

(1st April 2013)

12

'NEWBORNS'

(The Circle opens with the Sounds of the Tibetan bowls and the Crystal bowls.)

Let the resonance of the bowls sit within your Hearts, uplifting the Light and the Love deep within you, allowing you to soar into your Soul Dimension, for it is within your Soul Dimension that you will now perceive the world around you, and perceive your own place within that world.

I greet you, Dear Hearts, I am Hilarion.

I come tonight to say to you, this is not a time for standing still! This is not a time for letting go of your dreams and your visions! There are times we know that you feel disappointed that things within your world are not moving forward at the pace that you would like, at the pace that you assumed would happen after the Great Shift, but remember, Dear Hearts, when you were small, when you came into this world in this lifetime and started to look around and see magnificent things, you were not in a position to grasp those magnificent things, because you still had growing to do.

Most of you here will, at some stage, have learned to swim, but you did not do so by leaping into the centre of the ocean and expecting to make it to shore. No, you started small, perhaps a few yards out into the pool and back to the side, and each day as you grew in confidence, and you grew in assurance of your own abilities, you began to move further and further until you could go from one side of the pool to the other.

Some of you may have been quite content with that, and got out of the pool and walked away, others however sought to learn more, and to do more until indeed, they were able to step into the ocean and swim quite some distance.

Well, Dear Hearts, you have moved into a new Dimension, you are *'newborns'* once more, and there are magnificent things that you are seeing, that you are feeling, which you are not yet able to grasp, because you have learnings to do within this new Dimension, you have to learn once more how to swim in this new 'Ocean of Oneness'.

You see, the Dimension of Oneness, Dear Hearts, is quite different to the Dimension of separation. You have to learn new skills, new understandings, you have to work with different aspects of yourself, aspects that were undeveloped in the old Dimensions, but are so important in the Dimension of Oneness.

You need to learn to work from within your Hearts, to perceive everyone and everything upon the Earth Planet as part of yourself, and amplify the knowing within yourself that whatever you think, whatever you feel, and whatever you do ripples out and connects, and becomes a part of everyone else, and everything else upon the Earth.

This is quite different from being separate, Dear Ones. It is a whole new Ocean. So this is not the time to stop, this is not the time to give up simply because you are not seeing the progress that you are making. It is indeed a time to intensify the intent within your Hearts and within your minds, and to embrace this new Ocean of Oneness.

Imagine yourself once more as a newborn, looking at the world through new eyes, reaching out, touching, feeling with new senses, for being in 'Oneness' is much more than the physical senses you have experienced and worked with previously, *the Dimension of Oneness encompasses ALL your senses.*

Yes, in the old Dimension there was some talk perhaps of a sixth sense. The sixth sense is but the start. You are opening to more and more ways of sensing and seeing, and perceiving, and knowing the Earth on which you live.

You are a Cosmic Being, a Multidimensional Being. You are no longer limited by those senses you used in the Dimension of separation. You are a newborn. Look out upon the world - this new Dimension of Oneness - with the wonder of a newborn.

You see, a newborn has no limitations, they have not learned to limit themselves, and this Dear Hearts is what we are inviting you to do now, not to limit yourself anymore, but to simply open yourself to the experiences of this new Dimensional frequency.

There will be energies coming in from Cosmic sources to assist and aid you in this new endeavour, some may be a little like the floatation devices you may have started your swimming with. They are designed to assist you; they are not designed to entrap you. This is the Dimension of Oneness.

Open your Hearts, look at the world through your Hearts, not through your eyes, or through your minds, but through your Hearts, and embrace every Being, every creature upon the Earth as a part of you, and you begin to feel the difference, and you begin to open to a new wonderment, and you begin to reach out to touch, to feel, to embrace and to create a wondrous New Earth.

Dear Hearts, do not lose hope. Do not be despondent if the world does not move as fast as you would like it to move. You need to crawl before you can walk, and you need to walk before you can run. This you know, but for this moment you are a newborn.

Look at the world through the eyes of a newborn, see it as infinite possibilities, and take it into your

Heart and mould it. Mould it with Love and you will grow more quickly than you ever imagined.

I bless you, Dear Hearts, and I look forward to being with you on your journey. I too see the New Earth through the eyes and the Heart of a ***NEWBORN!***

(6th May 2013)

13

SHAMBHALA OF EARTH MOTHER'S HEART

(The Circle opens with the Sounds of the Tibetan bowls, the Blessings Chimes and the bell.)

As a Circle of Light and Love, on the waves of Sound from the Blessings Chimes, we shift in Dimensional Frequencies and embrace the Shambhala at the Heart of Earth Mother. Feel yourselves surrounded by the Crystalline Light Grid, and absorb the powerful Light energies that exist within your Soul Dimension in the Shambhala of Earth Mother, and feel yourselves empowered completely by the Divine Love within the Crystalline Grid, within the Heart of Earth Mother, and within the Soul Heart of each and every one of you within this Circle.

FEEL the Love, BE the Love, and feel yourself expanding, reaching out through your Hearts to embrace the whole of Humanity, sharing your Light and your Love and inviting every Being upon the Earth and within the Earth, to join your ever expanding Circle of Light in your Soul Dimensional Frequencies in the Shambhala of Earth Mother's Heart.

Greetings Dear Hearts, I am Hilarion.

I welcome you to your new abode within the Shambhala of Earth Mother's Heart, for this place, Dear Hearts, was your beginning, and now it will be your new frequency of Light for the remainder of your journey upon the Earth Planet, for *you have reconnected in your Soul Dimension to the infinite grace of the Creator, through the Heart of Earth Mother.*

You have been separated from Earth Mother for far too long and the time is now right for you to resume your connection with Earth Mother and to feel yourselves surrounded once more by her Divine Feminine Love.

Listen to the beat of her Heart as it vibrates through every fibre of your Being, listen to the Sounds of Divine Love resonating through the Crystalline Grid, connecting to the crystalline aspects of your own Being.

You began your existence within the Heart of Earth Mother and you moved to the surface of the Earth Planet to experience new beginnings, new challenges, new lessons and in time you forgot where you came from, but now the veil of forgetfulness is withering away, for as you move back into your Hearts you find yourself responding to the call of Earth Mother's Heart.

Now you have returned to re-experience the Shambhala, the meeting place of Souls deep within the Heart of Earth Mother. Feel the Love, feel the Peace, feel the Joy as you are embraced anew by beloved Earth Mother, for she has never forgotten you even though you may have forgotten her, for *a mother never forgets her child and you are all children of Earth Mother's Heart,* part of the Crystalline Grid, part of every facet of Earth Mother's Being.

As you experience this reunion of Hearts, know that from this time forth you will be radiating the Light and the Love of Earth Mother, and all Beings upon the Earth will feel and know this new Love Energy that you have embraced tonight.

Align your own heartbeat with that of Earth Mother and radiate forth Soul Love, Soul Peace and Soul Joy. All the creatures on the Earth, all the trees and the plants upon the Earth, all will receive this new vibrational frequency through you from the Heart of Earth Mother.

Take your time, enjoy being the Love, enjoy being the Peace and when you emerge from the Shambhala at the Heart of Earth Mother know that you will be changed, your Light will be brighter, your Energy will be more powerful, and all those around you will know that you are now completely

ONE WITH THE EARTH PLANET.

(22nd February 2016)

14

NO ONE ENSLAVES
YOU ANY MORE

(The Circle opens with the Sounds of the Tibetan
Bowls and the Blessings Chimes)

Feel the energies of the words just spoke.

Open to the Love within yourself.
Open to the Light within yourself.
Open to the Joy within yourself.

Allow that Love, that Light and that Joy to become
the means by which you perceive the world around
you – the means by which you see into other Beings
around you.

Through the Love, and the Light, and the Joy within
yourself, see the Love and the Light and the Joy
within others.

But most of all, feel those energies within yourself and within others, for you are moving into a Dimensional Frequency where 'Feeling' takes over from 'seeing'. For 'feeling' is the means by which your 'Heart' expresses itself to you.

I greet you Beloveds, for I am Hilarion.

I come tonight to speak briefly on a matter of considerable importance. It is about *'perceptions'* – for the changing of perceptions is part of the journey that you are currently undertaking, as the world that you know changes before your very eyes.

It does so because you are changing, and therefore perceiving the world around you through 'different' eyes, and through the 'feelings' within your Hearts.

I wish to speak to you about *'lifetimes'*.

For many of Humanity the awareness that you have lived many lifetimes upon your Planet is uplifting and freeing, as it takes away the fear of what you call 'death'.

You begin to recognize that you are on a journey of many parts. You have chosen to be on this Planet as part of that journey at this time, and at other times.

But the Planet on which you have existed until this time has been a Planet of *'linear time'*. So each occasion you have chosen to journey within this Dimensional system, you have moved back into 'linear time', so you perceive your many journeys upon this Earth in the context of that Linear time – as, if you like, continuous.

There are, Dear Hearts, two sides to every coin. On one side of this coin is the upliftment and the freeing from knowing that you are on a long journey, interspersed with periods on this Planet, and periods off this Planet, but still a life that is continuous.

On the opposite side of the coin, however, is enslavement. You may ask yourself "How could this be?". The reality is, Dear Hearts, that those who have sought control over others within your Dimension have utilized this concept of multiple lives to create chains to enslave you! It has been given many names, such as karma, and many of your Religions speak of this. They create the perceptions of good and bad, of sin and restitution.

Even with the enlightenment that has come with this knowing of many portions of your lives, you have been enslaved by the concepts that you somehow have to atone for what you have done in previous existences on this plane.

So you see, you have been freed on one side, and enslaved on the other!

Dear Hearts, when you move from this Dimensional existence on your Earth, you do not take the duality of this place with you. You move into the Unity of the Creator energy, and you embrace the lifetime you have just spent on the Earth. You do not judge that as good or bad, you simply acknowledge its existence and determine the extent to which you have grown from that experience.

Then you ask yourself if you wish to return to this place for further growth, or for some purpose consistent with the growth of the Earth herself.

Most of you have come in this lifetime to be of Service to the Earth and its 'transition', and yet many of you are still bound and enslaved by these perceptions of having to atone for past existences. This is an illusion deliberately created in the Human Consciousness to hold you in the third Dimensional Frequencies.

It is imperative, Dear Ones, that you let go of these chains! that you acknowledge that what is past, has past! It has been dealt with in the Unity of the Creator energy in your in-between times!

There is no residual! that is the illusion that those that are in control wish you to have!

It is time to unshackle yourself, and to exercise the freedom within your Heart – The freedom to work with the full power of your energy on your purpose for being here at this time. *To Enlighten the Earth through your own Enlightenment.*

Release these concepts that control.
Set yourself free.

You are answerable to yourself for all that you do within this Journey – not past journeys, Dear ones, This Journey.

Once you acknowledge, realize and accept that this is so, a great burden is lifted from your shoulders, and your Angelic wings are able to grow, lifting you into higher Dimensional frequencies.

Release yourself, and you begin to release the Consciousness of Humanity from this enslavement - this control. Reach into your Hearts, Dear Ones. Embrace the Love, the Light and the Joy that is within you. Look around you. Shine your Light.

No one enslaves you any more!

I thank you for listening, my blessings be upon you.

Feel yourself uplifted and enlightened, and feel the doors to other Dimensions open wide. Embrace the wisdom of those who wish to share at this time.

> *Embrace your new freedom.*
> *Embrace your New Earth,*
> *Embrace the LOVE.*

And so it is.

(4th April 2011)

15

HELPING TO BUILD A HEAVEN ON EARTH

(The Circle opens with the Sounds of the Tibetan bowls and the 'Cosmic Tone')

Feel the upliftment of the Sound Frequencies, allow yourselves to float within its embrace, lifting you upwards to your Soul Dimension, and take the time to sit a while in that Soul Dimension, and to look out upon your life from a highest perspective of Being.

Greetings Dear Hearts, I am Hilarion.

You have received many messages over many months and years of your Earth time that speak of the changes that are, and will be, taking place upon the Earth Planet, and changes invariably result, within humanity, in *'expectations'*.

You look at the changes that are taking place, and you have 'expectations' of what will be created. You may even choose to add your energy to particular creations, and then you forget that you are but one small part of the whole, and it is the energy of the whole that is creating the realities that result from those changes.

So what you see when those changes take place may not be what you as an individual portion of the whole had expected, and as is customary with Humans, you feel frustrated.

Things are not going the way you planned, hmm? You feel frustrated. You may perceive that you have taken two steps forward and one step back, or even one step forward and two steps back if you are feeling particularly negative, and you feel frustrated, and if you sit and wallow in that frustration, you cease to dream your dream.

So it is important for the changes that are taking place on the Earth at this time, that you find a way to recapture your dream and to dream that dream afresh. It is time to move into your Soul Dimension and to take the panoramic view of what is happening upon the Earth.

Perhaps I can express it in this way – when you determine to build a house, it does not all come together at one time, first you have to create the foundations, and when your foundations are in place, you then have to lay out your concrete slab, and when that is set and anchored you then begin to build upon that, the structure of your house, and as the walls go up and the rooms are created, if you are looking only at a single storey house, then place a roof upon it. It is not until that has been completed that you have the house you perceived at the beginning.

If you choose to have a two storey house, you cannot create the second storey until, and unless you have anchored the first storey effectively, solidly, to enable it to hold the second storey. And then again, you can put the roof on and you have a place where you can live, and it may be precisely the house you dreamed in your dreams, or it may only be a part of what you dreamed, because in building this house you have consulted with others, with engineers and you have made certain changes along the way, so what has been completed was not your original dream, and as you stand back and look upon this house you have the choice to feel frustrated, that it was not as you initially perceived, or you can look at the house and be grateful for the contribution of others, and feel joyful at the outcome of what has been created.

Over recent times, Dear Hearts, you have participated in accepting the inflow of new energies into your Earth, and you have been asked to anchor those energies into the Earth. Perhaps you have expected immediate results, and have not perceived those immediate results and have therefore felt frustrated, but as with the house you first have to establish the foundations, and then you have to lay the concrete slab and wait for that concrete slab to set.

In other words, Dear Hearts, you have to anchor those energies into the Earth and into your Hearts, and when they are set, when they are ready to be built upon there is a new inflow of energy, and once more you are asked to assist in the anchoring of those energies, so that the next part of the journey can begin, and each of you, through your Hearts, will help to anchor that new inflow of energy, and again you may expect immediate results and you do not perceive them, for you are still embracing your linear thinking, and your linear feelings.

I am saying to you, Dear Hearts, at those moments of doubt, of frustration take the time to float upwards on those Sound Frequencies and to sit within your Soul Dimension and to look out upon the Earth and see how it is changing, how the new structures of the Earth are beginning to appear. They may not look like what you thought they would look like, they may not even look completed, but because you are looking from a higher perspective, you are not feeling those frustrations.

You know in this higher perspective that all is moving according to plan, and you give thanks for having been a part of what has been created to this time, and know that more and more energy will be coming to the Earth, and more and more Light Workers will be anchoring those energies and helping to build the 'mansion' that has been called 'Heaven' - a Heaven on Earth.

Each one of you will have a different vision, a different dream, a different perception of how this 'Heaven' will look, but when it comes fully into Being, you will be amazed at its beauty. It will be vastly greater that you had ever anticipated, and yet within your Hearts you already know that it will be totally magnificent, filled with Love and Peace and Harmony.

Shortly you will again anchor energies into the Earth to create, or to release from previous bondage, **8 additional Dimensions of the Earth**. Do not try in your minds to imagine what this would look like, simply embrace the energies with Love, and Sound them into the Earth and allow the 'mansion' to be created by the Sounds of Love from your Hearts.

Let go of your frustrations

   Embrace the Joyfulness

   Embrace the Love

     Embrace the Earth, and BE the Creator/ God that you are.

(7th October 2013)

16

WE ARE IN AWE OF THE ILLUMINATION RADIATING FORTH FROM THE EARTH PLANET

(The Circle opens with the Sounds of the Tibetan Bowls and the Blessings Chimes)

Greetings Beloveds, I am Hilarion.

If you could but see the Illumination that has taken placed within the Ocean Consciousness of your Planet, you would be in awe as we are. The whole of the Earth is vibrating with a frequency of Light never before seen throughout the Cosmos.

The beautiful Beings of Light within the Ocean Consciousness are singing songs of great joy and they become filled with this new Light of Illumination.

As for Humanity, and the Humanity Consciousness, there is just a glimmer of the Awakening of Enlightenment, and as this year progresses in your linear time, this Enlightenment will become more and more obvious throughout the Earth, and as the Humanity Consciousness takes upon itself the energies of Enlightenment, it will begin to meld more deeply with the Illumination of the Ocean Consciousness.

It is the duty of the Oceans at this time, to hold this Light frequency of Illumination and Enlightenment, and to embrace Humanity progressively, allowing them - in the fullness of their time - to become filled with this new and powerful Light of understanding.

As Humanity awakens to the Enlightenment of themselves, they will begin to create the world that has been prophesised - the world of Peace - the world of Love - the world of Harmony.

The many Beings of Light who have moved to other Dimensional Frequencies of the Earth will once more come into your awareness; will once more communicate their Light, and their Love, adding it to the Illumination of the Ocean Consciousness.

If you look now, Dear Ones, through your Hearts at the Oceans of your Planet, you will see them vibrate with a different frequency. You will see them in their ***illumined*** state, and you will be in awe of what has taken place.

You, Dear Ones, through your open Hearts, have created this change. It is not something that is imposed from above, from outside your Planet - oh yes, there are many Beings of Light surrounding your Planet at this time - waiting, watching, ready to embrace you with their Love.

This will not happen until your Hearts are sufficiently opened to be able to acknowledge and respect their differences, and as the old energies of the third dimensional frequencies fade and dissolve, your Hearts will open more, and you will see more. You will see into other Dimensional Frequencies, and you will reach out with Love in your Heart - not with the fear of the past - and you will embrace the many Beings of Light throughout the Cosmos that come to you in Love.

For Love is always the key to Awakening. You cannot awaken when you are surrounded by the shadows of fear, when you are wrapped in the energies of anger.

Love creates a Peacefulness, a Joyfulness, and as you look through your Hearts and see the Earth through your Hearts, and see other Beings of Light through your Hearts, the Light frequencies will rise and rise, and you will become one with the illumined Ocean Consciousness.

Dear Hearts, we have worked together for eons of time, and we are coming to the end of one journey and the beginning of another.

Do not be afraid.

Do not be afraid of change.

Embrace it.

Welcome it into your lives.

For as you radiate the Light within your Hearts, you begin to change all that is around you.

It is time to let go of the old ways of focusing on what you do not have, instead of expressing gratitude for what you do have. What is created within your world is created by your thoughts and your feelings.

So focus not on the negatives, focus instead on the gratitude and the Love and the Light that is within your own Hearts, but also surrounds you.

Look for that Light in everyone you meet. Too often in the past you have looked to the shadows in others. It is time, Dear Ones, to look only for the Light, and to welcome that Light and express your gratitude for that Light, for the sharing, for the harmonising of the frequencies of the Earth.

Take time to spend a little time during your day beside the Ocean. Close your eyes and open your Hearts and see the glow of Illumination, and feel the embrace of the vibration of Harmony, and allow that to empower you, that each step that you take in this year to come may build on the one before, uplifting, creating Light within yourself to share with others.

I say again Dear Ones, we are in awe of what you have achieved.

We are in awe of the Illumination that is radiating forth from the Earth Planet.

Embrace it.

Empower it within yourself, and reach out to all those who share that Light of Love.

I embrace you with the Light of my Love, and I thank you.

(26th March 2012)

17

ENABLING OTHERS TO FIND THE LIGHT WITHIN THEMSELVES

(The Tibetan and Crystal bowls Sound.)

Focus on your Heart Chakra, reaching deep within your Heart and embracing the core Light of your Being. See yourself turning up that Light, allowing it to flood your Heart with the highest vibrational frequencies you possess - the frequency of Divine Love and Divine Peace.

As you raise your Light within your Heart, feel the Light of your higher self flowing down through your thymus and connecting with the Light within your Heart, bringing into oneness all aspects of your multidimensional self.

You are now in a time of Unity and Oneness. You have moved through the Portal of Transformation and you have left behind the realm of separateness. Embrace your oneness with your higher self. Embrace your oneness with the higher selves of all those within the room. Feel the power of that oneness, and know that the Light of that oneness is spreading out across the world, and out into the Cosmos.

As you focus upon the Light within your Heart, you become the Light within the Earth, and as you become the Light within the Earth you become the Light within the Cosmos, for all are one.

I greet you Beloveds, I am Hilarion.

You have over the last few weeks of your time, been adjusting your energy patterns to the inflow of Cosmic energies that took place at the 11.11.11 - the inflow of the energy of **understanding**.

As you have been told, enlightenment only occurs when wisdom is aligned with understanding, and you all have a fountain of wisdom within yourselves.

The energies that are flowing into the Planet at this time are the energies to enable you to understand the wisdom within yourselves, and through this process, to become enlightened beyond measure.

It takes time for those that are in the lower Dimensions to adjust to these frequencies of Light that the Cosmos are gifting the Earth at this time.

You have been in a period of rest and recuperation, and again you have been advised to make use of this time by not seeking always to ground yourself into the Earth, but to lift yourself up into the higher vibrational frequencies, to allow the Cosmic energies to lift you up, that you may have a greater perspective on your journey.

That time of rest and recuperation is coming to an end, for at the time of the Solstice there will be another inflow of the Cosmic energies of understanding.

You have recently witnessed a total eclipse of the moon. This was a key, unlocking the understanding, aligning it with the wisdom.

As you move towards the special inflow of energy, you will be awakened more and more, and you will begin to see your journey in a greater Light than ever before, and you will find yourself giving greater Love than ever before – Divine Love - Unconditional Love.

Those energies amplified through the Light in your Heart will spread across the Planet, enabling others to awaken to the Light within themselves.

This is no longer a time of people changing people. It is a time simply of enabling others to find the Light within themselves.

By projecting your Light out into the world, you give a lead, you provide a blueprint, you connect to the Hearts of those who are yet to awaken, and you allow those people, those Beings of Light - that do not know they are of the Light - to find that Light within themselves.

There may be those who come to you for help and assistance, because they see the amazing Light that you project, and I urge you to give that assistance in all ways, respecting their right to grow from within.

Feel the Light within yourself now. Feel it grow. Feel it flow. Accept and embrace the higher wisdom, the higher understanding that will lead you to a state of Enlightenment.

At the time at the next Marine Meditation you will walk the Labyrinth of Inner Vision, and you will pass through the Portal of Enlightenment, for by that time you will have aligned wisdom with understanding, and you will begin to create a world that you have dreamed of for eons of time.

There is no going back. There is only upliftment, an enhancement of the energies within your own Heart, *an alignment with your higher self – your own inner vision.*

Feel the power of the Love within this Circle at this time, know that you are *One* with each other, know that you are *One* with many around the Earth at this time, and you will become *One* with many, many more as the enlightenment and the upliftment spreads and spreads, reaching into the darkest corners of the Earth and sharing the Light of Hope, the Light of Love.

I bless you and embrace you, and I thank each and every one of you for the work that you do to assist in this transformational process. *Embrace yourselves with Love, for you are worthy of your own Love.*

The Tibetan and Crystal bowls sound.

Let the drum reflect the heart beat of the Circle.

Let the energy of abundance be with each and every one of you.

And so it is.

(12th December 2011)

18

YOU ARE ALL HUMAN RAINBOWS

(The Tibetan bowls Sound)

Greetings, Dear Hearts, I am Hilarion

Feel the vibration of those Sounds shaking loose the final residual embers of the past, releasing them into the Light, and allowing greater Light to flow into your Being, to illuminate the essence of your Being, to uplift and embrace the joyfulness of all that is.

You have allowed yourselves to fly like the butterfly through the Light of the Cosmos that is flowing to the Earth at this time, creating within yourself the transformation of separateness into Unity - a Unity within yourself, and a Unity within the Consciousness of Humanity.

As you move forward, it is time to embrace your brothers and sisters with Love and Light and Peace and Respect. For now, more than ever, *what you do to others - you do to yourself*, for you have accepted and embraced the Unity of all that is, the Oneness of your Consciousness of Humanity, and your Consciousness within the Planet Earth.

Love yourself, and let that Love flow to others around you. Draw them into your circle of Light, and bless them with your joy - for we are all One.

Feel the Light quotient within each cell of your Being increase dramatically, as you begin to explore the Oneness that you have become.

Your journey of separateness is over, but you will need to learn and to practice, being the Oneness of all that is.

Feel the pulsations of Light from the Cosmos beating within your Heart, forming a wave of Light within you that you radiate forth, and that you Sound forth, proclaiming the oneness of all.

As you perceive others as being a part of yourself, you embrace them with greater Love and without judgement.

Feel the Light growing within you, increasing your understanding and your awareness. Feel your friends from beyond the veil gathering close within your Light, gifting you their strength of purpose, that you may walk this new path of Unity with ease and grace, with beauty and harmony, with Peace and Love.

Let your new sense of Oneness Sound forth.

It is time for you to recognise that you are all Human Rainbows, radiating your Light through many Dimensions, and many frequencies, but always part of the whole.

Listen to your inner Light and speak your truth.

Blessings be.

(26th September 2011)

19

BREATHE

(The Circle opened with the Sounds of the Tibetan Bowl, the Blessings Chimes and the Drum)

Greetings, Dear Hearts, I am Hilarion

Focus on your breathing, allow your breathing to become measured, neither too fast nor too slow, breathing in a way that compliments the beating of your Heart. You were reminded in the Meditations from Beloved Crystals and Gemstones to *'Breathe in, hold, Breathe out' – 'Breathe in, hold, Breathe out',* for it is the measured Breath that stills the mind and stills the body and allows you to open to other frequencies, other Dimensional Realms.

Breathe in, hold, breathe out. Feel yourself becoming totally relaxed and allow your mind to move its awareness to your Heart. so that the Heart Beat pulses within your mind and connects you in your understanding in your own Consciousness to the Centre of your Being.

The moment you connect to the Centre of your Being you feel an immense rush of powerful energies through your whole Physical Body. Every part of your Being seems to expand and you move beyond your Physical Vessel to embrace the vibrational Frequencies of the surrounding Dimensions – the Dimensions of your Soul, the Angelic Realms, within which are not merely the Angels, but a myriad of other Beings of many forms from many sources within the Cosmos, your Beloved Unicorns and Dragons all reside in the Angelic Realms of Light. You too reside in this Realm as a *Soul Being of Infinite Light and Infinite Love*. All is within the Centre of your Being, your Physical vessel is simply a part of the Whole.

It is time for you to acknowledge and accept and understand the Great Being that you are.

Feel the vibration of your Soul as it traverses time and space, as it draws into your energy field the vibrations of Sound and Light from every part of the Cosmos, from every part of the Inner Earth, for each is an important part of the Whole.

As you feel the expansion of your *'Self'*, reach out and embrace all those you meet as you move through the Dimensions, for you have moved past 'fear' into Pure Love, and in the purity of that Love you embrace all Beings. You do not embrace them as 'Masters' but as 'Friends', for in your greater understanding of yourself you recognize the Equality of all that is. You are as much a Master as those you look up to and respect in your Third Dimensional realities. Each one of you is a part of the *'SOURCE'*, so move with pride and confidence through all Dimensions, and embrace and acknowledge all other Beings of Light that you meet. Give and receive the energies of Love, for as you do so you empower the Light and Love within yourself.

Breathe in, hold, Breathe out - Breathe in, hold, Breathe out.

Now allow yourself to explore the wonderful world of your inner Song, a World of Equality, A World of Oneness, a meeting place of the Cosmic Brotherhood. Sound Vibrations are the connections between Souls. Allow your Heart to Sound your

Love, your Joy, your Peace, that others in the Cosmos may openly receive your gift.

When you moved into the Physical Dimension, you did not lose your Soul Heart, you merely lost your ability to see it, to feel it and to connect with it. But that time is past! now you are connected once more to your Soul Heart, and can move with ease between Dimensions, and you will do this more and more as the Gateways, the Star Gates into your Soul Hearts are open, and remain open.

Let go of all things that do not support your connection with your Soul Heart, and enjoy this new stage of your Journey into your Soul.

I am Hilarion, and I bless you with much Love.

BREATHE IN, HOLD, BREATHE OUT – BREATHE IN, HOLD, BREATHE OUT – BREATHE IN, HOLD. BREATHE OUT.

And so it is.

(10th August 2009)

20

YOUR HEART IS THE RECEPTOR
OF LIGHT AND SOUND

(The Circle opens with the Sounds of the Tibetan
Bowls and the Blessings Chimes)

Feel yourselves floating upwards on the Frequency
of the Blessings Chimes, moving through different
Dimensional aspects of yourself, lifting yourself
higher and higher until you become fully the
Oneness that you really are, when you no longer
feel the separation from others within the Circle, but
you feel the Oneness of all that is.

Take some time, Dear Hearts, to sit within the
embrace of that Oneness the Highest Dimensional
Frequency of Humanity. Feel the Love, Feel the Joy
and BE the Peace.

Greetings. Dear Hearts, I am Hilarion

I Thank you for inviting me into your Oneness that we may share together the uniqueness of each individual as a part of the wholeness, for we all exist in a state of Oneness in the highest levels of Frequency and Dimension. It is as if you are sitting in Council with each other, and in Council with the Masters, and the Angels, and all the other Beings of Light, Cosmic Beings of Light, Earthly Beings of Light, who desire to share their wisdom with your Hearts, *for it is through your Hearts, and not your minds, that you absorb the greatest wisdom.* For the greatest wisdom is not contained within the words, it is contained within the vibrational Frequencies of Light and Sound - *and your Heart is the receptor of Light and Sound.*

The Blessings Chimes have elevated you into this new state of Consciousness, this new awareness of Sound and Light that encompasses the whole of the Earth Planet, the whole of the Universe, the whole of the Cosmos. Simply allow yourselves to feel this upliftment of Light and Sound within your Heart, and let your Hearts speak to one another, embrace one another, Revel in the Joy of Oneness.

When you come together in Circle you let go of the old, and you embrace the new - the new Light, the new Sound, the new Frequencies of *Love* and *Joy*, and when you walk from this Circle you do so elevated in Spirit, and you shine your own Light more brightly to others upon the Earth, and you communicate with others through your Light, through your Sound.

Words have been constructed upon the Earth to communicate, but the greatest communication of all is simply the ***ENERGY OF LOVE*** that reaches out from deep within your Being, carried on the waves of Sound and the Frequencies of Light, and you touch everything around you with no words, simply with the vibration of Love and the Frequency of Joy,

It is important, Dear Hearts, to recognize that you *Are* Divine Beings and you communicate through your Hearts. Although words have become important they are not the 'be all and end all' of life, *that,* Dear Hearts, is Frequency of Light.

You are now approaching a new year in your linear time, and it will not be a year that is the same as the one before, for the Frequency of your Light has changed. You have absorbed the Sound Vibrations from Arcturus in the period from your Equinox to your Solstice, you have taken those Sound Vibrations within your Heart and transmuted them into the energy of Love and Peace within your material world. So you will step forth into your new linear year with a brighter Light, with a purer Sound, and you will be a clarion call to the rest of Humanity

They will hear your Sound, and they will feel your Light, and they will begin to change, they will begin to look for that Sound and that Light within themselves, for *like attracts like*, and the Love and the Joy and the Peace that you are radiating through your Sound and through your Light will be seeded in the Hearts of many, many more upon the Earth Planet, and as each Being awakens to the Divinity within themselves the Light Frequencies of the whole of the Earth will be elevated once more, more quickly than ever before.

The darkness, the separation, fades as more and more Light, and more and more Sound permeates the Earth, and every one upon it, and within it. There are still, Dear Hearts, many changes ahead of you, but these are changes that will elevate Humanity. It will push away the darkness, it will Sound away the anger and the hatred that has resided for too long upon the Earth, for the Light and the Sound are of Love and of Joy. ***Each time you sound your Blessings Chimes you are knocking on the door of someone's Heart, and they WILL open that door and allow the Light within their own Hearts to begin to emerge.***

Dear Hearts, we will all be with you, Sounding and embracing Humanity with our Love, and our Light. I look forward to the journey ahead.

(29th December 2014)

21

WE ARE ALL ENERGY BEINGS IN DIFFERENT FORMS

(The Circle opens with the Sounds of the Tibetan bowls and the Blessings Chimes)

Embrace the resonance of the Blessings Chimes and the Bowls, drawing them into your innermost Heart and allowing them to meld with every aspect of your Being so that the whole of your physical body becomes one Resonance in all Dimensional Frequencies of Self.

Greetings, Dear Hearts, I am Hilarion.

It is with great interest that we have listened to your discussions this evening, reawakening memories of the past - recent past and ancient past - for this is a time of coming together in Oneness, coming together in the *Now,* and acknowledging the true worth of Self. All the experiences of many lifetimes on the Earth Planet that each of you has undertaken, all is within you, not necessarily in the immediacy of your memory at this time, but the resonance of everything is contained within your Being.

Indeed, Dear Hearts, your Spirit friends come to visit in order to throw some Light upon some aspect of what you already know, for there is nothing that you do not know, it is always, Dear Hearts, a question of relevance to the time and the place within this physical aspect of your journey, for you have created the linear time in which you live, and within that linear time only certain aspects of your knowledge are necessary to be at the forefront of your mind, but from time to time it is important to draw from deep within yourselves the knowledge and the wisdom that you have always had, for from time to time it is necessary to share that wisdom with others around you, with others across the world, so that you may do the job that we do with you, casting a Light on some part of someone's journey, allowing them to draw from within their own knowing that which is necessary for this part of their journey.

You see, Dear Hearts we are all Guides, one to another, we are all a part of the One. Feel the joy within you, as in this moment you fully embrace the wondrous Being that you are, acknowledging your Light, your wisdom, but most of all, acknowledging your Resonance, for as you have been reminded this evening, *it is your resonance that is important in how you relate to others, how you relate to the Planet, how you relate to the Cosmos.*

We are all Energy Beings in different forms, and when we speak of Higher or Lighter, we are simply referring to different aspects of our own resonance. When you play a single note on your piano, if you listen carefully, focus carefully, you will hear the many harmonies within that one note - *that is the resonance. Resonance moves through all your Dimensional Frequencies, it is your multidimensionality manifesting.*

In meditation you often move into different Frequencies of Self, frequencies is another of your terms for resonance. All frequencies are contained within the single note - all resonance is contained within the single Being.

We speak to you of Light, of radiating forth your Light, that is your resonance as much as Sound is your resonance. It is a term you do not use often enough when speaking of yourselves, Dear Hearts, but tonight you have been reminded of that and you may wonder why, but you only have to go back to the message you received last week from beloved Sananda to know the importance of focusing on your resonance as you move towards the Solstice, when the earth will be bathed in the Magenta Light. The Magenta Light is a part of the resonance of the Earth Planet, it is a different frequency of Light, a different frequency, a different colour, a different Sound, but all a part of the Whole.

Take time whenever you can to move deep into your Heart and focus the *'resonance of your Being'* on the Earth Planet as a whole, and you will immediately be connected to the Heart of the Earth, and your Heart will beat with the Heart of the Earth, you will be in a oneness, a Unity of Resonance.

There are so many variations of frequencies within resonance, reflected in Colour and Sound, reflected in Light, reflected in Emotions - the most powerful of which Dear Hearts is always **Love. Love is the** *highest of the resonance of the Earth and of all life forms upon the Earth.*

Embrace it, express it, **BE THE LOVE**, for when you are Love you become Peace, and you radiate the Magenta Light,

THE SPIRITUAL RESONANCE OF HEAVEN.

(11th May 2015)

22

SOUND THE BLESSINGS CHIMES

(The Circle opens with the Sounds of the Tibetan Bowl, the drum and the Blessings Chimes.)

We Sound the Blessings Chimes for the healing of all those who need healing within their Hearts at this time, for everything begins within the Heart. We Sound the Blessings Chimes for those who are ready to depart this life and continue their journey amongst the Stars, and we Sound the Blessings Chimes to greet those who have chosen to come to the Earth at this time, to BE in Oneness, to BE a new Light upon and within the Earth.

Allow the Blessings Chimes to move deeply within your Hearts and lift the energy of Joy to the surface of your Being and to the surface of the Earth, for it indeed is a time for bringing Joy to the forefront of relationships upon the Earth Planet, and in particular the relationship between Humanity and the Earth itself, for in Joyfulness you will seek only what is best for all.

The energies of greed, the energies of power one over another, have no place in the New Magenta Earth, so the Blessings Chimes also ring out a farewell to those old energies that disconnected and separated Humanity and the Earth.

Greetings, Dear Hearts, I am Hilarion.

It is a difficult time for those of us who have worked with you for so long, for like yourselves we are facing *'the empty page of the future'* and are seeking to create a new vibrational frequency for ourselves that we may continue to assist your growth in the new frequencies of Light, the New Magenta Earth.

This will very much be, Dear Hearts, a journey of mutual discovery, of mutual growth, but as has already been said – the essence of the future is the energy of Joy, and Joy can only well from deep within your own Hearts.

Joy has never been a state of mind, it has always been a state of Heart, and you know this, Dear

Ones, for in the old world you had a saying when someone was not Joyful about something, that *'they did not have their Heart in it'*. You never said 'they didn't have their mind in it', is that not so Dear Ones? *They didn't have their Heart in it,* so really, deep down, Dear Ones you have always known that the Heart is the guiding force of your existence, the guiding force of Humanity's collective existence, the guiding force of the Earth itself, and now that the Earth has opened her Heart, and filled every Being of Light upon the Earth with the Magenta Light, more and more you will find that it is the energy of Joy that will guide your every move.

You will continue to find problems in your way, for that is what Humans do, they seek and they find problems because they are so accustomed to the mind wishing to resolve problems, but now in this new Earth it is the Heart that will guide your decisions, and your decisions will be based on how much Joy would such an action bring to me and to others.

It will not be enough, Dear Hearts, for your actions to only bring Joy to yourself, for you have become a community in more ways than you realise. Every action you take, every decision you take, involves the rest of Humanity and involves Earth Mother. So you will no longer make rational decisions based on logic of the mind, you will make decisions based purely on how your Heart fills with Joyfulness - that will be the sole judgment of what is right and what is wrong for you, for the Earth, and for Humanity.

The criteria for all your decisions will be – *"Is this creating Joy for all?"* Of course, Dear Hearts, you continue to have free will, so you cannot always guarantee that others will be as Joyful about your decisions, but that should not draw you back into the logic of the mind, for if you are truly making your decision based on what your Heart feels is Joyful for all, then you are being true to yourself, and the future of the Earth Planet is about truth - *being true to your Heart.*

The Heart is much more than just the emotion of Love, the Heart determines the truth of YOU.

There will continue to be many ups and downs and many changes in life upon your Planet, for you are creating a new world, a new 'Community of Oneness'. The interaction between Humans and between Humans and the Earth Planet will gradually become indivisible. Your sense of Oneness will grow and grow until it becomes an automatic function of living, your judgments when you are faced with situations on your Earth will be purely one of Joyfulness, for if your actions do not bring you Joy and do not give the potential for Joy to others, you will know that those actions are not appropriate.

This will be a vast change attitudinally upon your Planet, so take your time, go deep within your Heart and be guided by the truth of Joy within YOU.

(3rd August 2015)

23

THE MIND IS THE FOUNDATION ON WHICH WE BUILD THE MANSION OF OUR HEART

(The Circle begins with the Sounds of the Tibetan Bowls, the Blessings Chimes and the Drum)

I think it is important for us all to realize that when we begin our journey of awakening we are shown, and we are given, information that is specific to our intellectual understanding of things. In other words, we are given information, we are given wisdom, we are given knowledge that our minds can understand, because our minds – like computers – are things of order and logic, and they can not comprehend, and they can not work with concepts that do not fit into these baskets, if you like to put it that way. It is only when we start to move into our Hearts that we open ourselves to the wisdom that defies the logic of the mind, and we start to understand our journey from a totally different perspective, and it is, as Krista says, the perspective of **Love.**

We start to let go of the threads of fear, and we dissolve those threads of fear with more and more Love, and as we embrace more and more Love we begin to receive information and wisdom more appropriate to our Hearts than to our minds.

So those rules we were given to begin with are rules that the mind can comprehend, and therefore the mind allows you to continue your journey. If we immediately jumped into the Heart aspect without going through the mind first, the mind, because of its protective mechanism of this world, would simply shut down and not allow us to operate.

So, Spirit, in its wisdom, speaks first to the mind and to the logic to gradually build a stage on which we can then begin to perform from the Heart. That does not mean that the wisdom we are given for our minds is wrong, it simply means that it is appropriate only for that period of time, and as we grow into our Hearts, we move into a higher understanding, and that wisdom and that logic becomes part of what we draw into our Hearts, and we see it differently. We see it with a totally different perspective.

Over the next two years we will be working with the Labyrinth that carries with it the Harmonic note of *EAGLE*. *Eagle is about seeing things from on high.* So, when we continue to work in our Hearts over the next two years, we will be seeing more and more of our lives, and more and more of our journeys from the higher perspective – the Heart and the Higher Self perspective.

The Mind has created the foundation, the Heart is now building the mansion. So there is no conflict between the mind and the Heart, as sometimes we tend to feel there is. *The Mind is simply the foundation on which we build the Mansion of the Heart.* When you can begin to see it that way, you begin to involve more and more of your Total Being, because all are part of the whole.

You do not discard the wisdom of your mind in order to work with the wisdom of your Heart, you embrace them both, you build on them both, because when you start to work more fully with your Heart, you then begin to reach more and more towards your Higher Self. You build that Mansion upwards, and as you build it upwards, you take on more and more Higher Perspective, more and more Higher Wisdom. Not the wisdom of others, but the wisdom of your Total Being. Yes you will still connect with others, you will still receive information from others, because others know different things to what you know.

Because you are expanding and embracing more and more of your Self, you are also embracing more and more of others, you are accepting and embracing the wisdom of others where it resonates with your Heart.

We have moved from Logic to Vision, and the Heart has the Vision, the Higher Self has the Vision. Build your Mansion at the Heart and see the Turret of that Mansion as your Higher Self. As you move into this Turret you see and connect with Beings in other Dimensional Frequencies. They become a part of you. Allow your mind to create pictures of this vision, the building of the mansion of your Heart, of moving through that mansion into the Turret.

You will notice that in all of your Religions throughout the world they build Mansions, and on those Mansions they build Turrets, and from those

Turrets they send forth Sound, whether it be the Bells of the Christian Religion, or the chants from the Minarets of the Muslim Religion

The higher you move, the greater you move with the Sound. You call out from your high pinnacle to other Beings of **Enlightenment**. It is within each one of us that we create those mansions and create those Turrets, and allow our perceptions of life to flow upwards to greet, to Sound forth, our wisdom. To share our Love at Higher levels.

Your Light calls out to others, just as they call out from the tops of the Churches with their Bells, or for the Imams with their chants, their calls to prayer. *You see, the call to prayer is simply the call to the enlightenment of your self. A call to you to uplift yourself into the energy of SOURCE.*

Although you have clothed these activities in Religious concepts and structures and rigid belief systems, the simple reality is that you are being called to **Your Source. You are being called into the Light, and you move into the Light through your Heart.**

Take a moment, imagine your own mansion built on the foundation of your mind, built on the substance of your Heart, reaching higher and higher into the ethers. Imagine yourself Sounding forth your Light, creating the call for more and more Light on your Planet, becoming the beacon of Light through **Sound**.

You may construct your Mansion in any form, in any colour. Allow your mind to exercise its creative faculties. See yourself becoming that Mansion, and as you move higher into the Turret, look around you, see your Spirit and other Friends waiting, reaching out with Love to greet you. Then allow yourself to look down upon your Planet, upon your Journey, your personal Journey into enlightenment.

As you see your journey from a Higher perspective, you release those cords of fear, you release all that is holding you back, you release through the energy of Love, dissolving those cords which hold you to the fear of the past, dissolving the cords through the energy of Love – *becoming free to Love even more*.

Release those cords of power that others have sought to enslave you with. Release them with Love and allow yourself to fully OWN your own power.

When you accept and acknowledge your own power, you increase your ability to share your Love with others, to share your Light with others, to share your Wisdom with others, for you acknowledge the equality of all that is.

Now move into your Turret and Sound forth your Love, your Joy, your Freedom.

Remember, Dear Ones, only you can build the Mansion of your Heart on the Foundation of your mind. Only you can lift that Turret up to your Higher Self. No one outside of yourself can build it – or break it down.

Embrace your own DIVINE POWER and BE THE LIGHT THAT YOU ARE

I am **Hilarion** and I Bless each and every one of you, and I thank you.

And so it is.

(4th October 2010)

24

EMBRACE THE 'SOURCE'
OF ALL LIGHT

(The Circle opens with the Sounds of the Tibetan Bowls and the Blessings Chimes)

Greetings, Dear Hearts, I am Hilarion

Focus on your Heart Chakra, but do not limit your perception of the Heart Chakra as being solely within the centre of your body, for your Heart Charka encompasses the whole of your physical and energetic Being.

As you move more and more into Heart energy, you become the Heart Chakra in its *full illumination*, expanding ever outwards, embracing all within your environment, until your Heart Chakra embraces the whole of the Earth Planet.

You become One with the Divine Love of Gaia, so as I say to you now, focus on your Heart Chakra, do so in this expanded form, welcoming, embracing the Heart energy of all that is.

Feel your wholeness with Gaia, and as you become comfortable focusing upon and embracing this expanded Heart Chakra within yourself, allow it to expand even more, moving out into the Cosmos, embracing and becoming one with the Sun and the Moon and the Planets, and as you become comfortable with that expansion, allow it to grow even more, and feel the energy of the Great Central Sun become a part of your Heart Chakra, resonating deeply within yourself; for you are not separate from any of these things, you are One. You are ONE with your Heart Energy.

Feel the beat of the Great Central Sun resonating through your whole Being. Feel the Power and the Light of the Divine Love within this expanded Heart Chakra, *know you are totally Love.*

As you feel and breathe and become 'total love', you see everything differently. You see in all things the Light that is emanating from within their Heart

Chakras, and you connect and become ONE, Heart to Heart - deeply, powerfully ONE with all that is.

Nothing that is within your understanding is separate from your Heart.

Feel the power of the Light within you.

Feel the vibration of Loving Sound within you.

Embrace beloved Gaia.

Embrace the Sun and the Moon and the Planets.

Embrace the Great Central Sun.

Embrace the 'Source' of all Light - the 'Source' of Divine Love.

Feel yourself begin to change in the vibrational frequency of your Being, becoming the essence of Divine Love, and communicating with all things and all Beings with the energy of Divine Unconditional Love.

Allow this expanded perception of the Heart Chakra to be the focus each and every day.

Let go of the limitations you have placed upon your Heart in the past.

Expand your knowing, and truly feel ONE with all that is.

(21st May 2012)

25

YOUR INNER SUN OF DIVINE LOVE

Just take a moment to embrace the energy of Beloved Mary, and also the energy of Beloved Quan Yin, and bring into your Hearts the energies of Divine Oneness.

(The Circle opens with the Sounds of the Tibetan bowl, the Crystal Bowl and the tingsha Bells.)

Focus on the vibrations of Sound flowing deep into the centre of your Being and awakening the flame of Divine Love within your Heart Chakra, and as you awaken this flame of Divine Love, empower it fully and totally with every aspect of your Being in this and all your other Dimensions, and see that flame of Divine Love grow brighter and brighter until it becomes the *Sun within your Heart*.

Feel the immense power of your Sun, your Inner Sun of Divine Love. Feel it pulse within your Being. Hear the Sound of your Inner Sun vibrating its frequencies of Love out into the Universe, and know that you are the centre of all life.

It is from within your Inner Sun that you are creating the changes taking place on your Earth at this time. Imagine the energies pulsing outwards from your Inner Sun, creating and recreating the realities around you, connecting to all the other Suns in the Universe, weaving golden threads of Light from one Sun to the next, creating the Cosmic flower of life - for life is created through Love.

See with your inner eye this Cosmic flower of Life as it becomes brighter and brighter and more powerful and more beautiful, and know that you are a source of this Flower of Life - a part of the whole.

Feel your Inner Sun begin to beat with the melody of Love within your Hearts, sending forth your threads of Golden Light, your patterns of Joy, your patterns of Light, your patterns of Sound, and feel your whole Being begin to vibrate with a new frequency of Light.

Guide that frequency of Light into the Earth itself and connect your Divine Love with the Heart Chakra of the Earth, and feel the responding vibration from the Earth returned to your Heart as a thread of Golden Light, of Joy.

Allow the connection to grow with each beat of your Inner Sun.

Feel the totality of oneness with the Earth, with the Cosmos, with all your brothers and sisters upon the Earth, and beyond the Earth.

Feel the magnificence of the energy of Divine Love, becoming the Oneness of all that is.

Now focus your beams of Light upon the Oceans of the world, connecting once more in Oneness with all the Light Beings of the Oceans, feeling the return of their Divine Love to you and embracing once more a Oneness of Spirit, a Oneness of purpose, a Oneness of Love.

I am Hilarion and I embrace you all with the Divine Love from the Inner Sun within me, and I share your Upliftment, your Illumination, your Enlightenment.

Send forth your Love.

Embrace all without judgement.

Embrace all with the Love from your Inner Sun.

(30th July 2012)

26

MUCH IS HAPPENING
BENEATH THE SURFACE

(The Circle opens with the Sounds of the Tibetan bowl, the Blessings Chimes and the drum.)

Greetings, Dear Hearts, I am Hilarion.

It is very easy at this time to feel confusion, for as you look out across your world you see great discord, chaos.

You see the Earth moving, expressing energy from deep within itself and it is easy for you to draw back inside your own Being and isolate yourself from what you perceive as the negativity that is happening upon your Planet. But this is not the time to be isolated, it is indeed a time to be working in *'Community' - one with another,* for within yourself you only see and feel and know a small part of what is happening, others will see and feel different parts of what is happening, so it is vitally important at this time of great change that you open your Hearts, you open yourselves and embrace those around you and invite those around you to share their wisdom, their knowledge with you, and you need to be prepared to share your wisdom and your knowledge with them.

Much is happening beneath the surface, beneath the surface of the Earth and also beneath the surface of Humanity's Consciousness. Much energy is flowing into the Earth at this time. You were told recently about the inflow of the *'Energy of Honey'* to enable the Earth and all the Light Beings on the Earth to be empowered even more in the *'Ocean of Love'*.

Your third dimensional bodies have at times been unable to accept and absorb these powerful energies, for they are intended to work at the highest frequency levels of your Being in your 'Soul Dimensions', so again it is important for you to be constantly uplifting your physical vessel into your Soul Dimension to enable these energies to be harmonised within the totality of your Being.

There is no longer a separation, Dear Hearts, between your Physical Dimension and your Soul Dimension, so consciously lift your physical vessel into your Soul Dimension and allow it to resonate with higher and higher frequencies of Light.

The energies you have just received from deep at the centre of your Cosmos is but one of a series of flows of energy that you have been receiving over recent times, over many years in fact in your linear time, and each time a new flow of energy comes in, the density of your physical Being has to adjust and absorb and balance and harmonise. For you see, Dear Hearts, the Earth itself is embracing these energies, *the Earth itself is moving into its Soul Dimension,* and yes the physicality that you see and feel of the Earth Planet also has to absorb, adjust, balance and harmonise with these energies, and sometimes, even the Earth Planet does not do this with ease and grace.

So when you feel discomfort with the inflow of these energies, do not blame yourself for this, accept that it is part of your process, part of your journey and simply focus on your Soul Dimension which now incorporates your Physical Dimension, and when the Earth Planet shows clearly that it is not coping with the new energies and it shakes and it rattles and it rolls, *do not blame the Earth Planet, embrace it with Love,* for through your Love you will assist the Earth Planet in uplifting itself into its own Soul Dimension, harmonising itself, balancing itself.

You have been told so many times, Dear Hearts, *"you are all ONE. and ONE with the Earth"*, and this is indeed so, so this is not a time for drawing back into yourself and isolating yourself, it is a time to open yourself more and more, opening your Hearts to all those upon the Planet and to the Earth Planet itself, and to share in the 'Living Soul Community' that *IS* the Earth at this time.

Your Spiritual friends have been gathered at Shambhala for quite some time and they have been opening their Hearts to embrace you and to embrace Earth Mother, to offer themselves as a part of the process of upliftment. *They are not drawing back into themselves as they see the challenges that the Earth is going through at this time,* no, Dear Hearts, they/we are opening ourselves even more to enable this upliftment to occur, and this is why we say to you – open yourselves more to enable the new energies to be absorbed and to be harmonised and as you do that you will feel this great upliftment within yourself and you will look around you and awaken to the *'Community of Love'* that is within this circle, and from this circle the connections that go out to embrace other circles around your country, around the world, for you are all connected as part of the *ONE* and the more of you that open and offer yourself totally and willingly to the enhancement of the process of ascension, the greater that ascension will be – but the more you pull back into yourself the more you will delay the inevitable ascension of Mother Earth and all those upon Mother Earth.

Again and again, Dear Hearts; we say to you – *"do not be judgmental, be accepting of others"*, for what you may perceive as weakness or wrong doing in others may in fact be an important part of their journey, of their ability to begin to awaken their Hearts and to open to the Love that is inherent within each and every one of you.

When you open your Heart to others, you encourage them to open also, but when you close your Heart to others you invite them to close their Hearts also.

We have said previously that this will be a year of choice, and the choice you have now is to open or to close, to embrace or to withdraw.

We ask you to choose wisely, to open your minds, to open your eyes, but most of all, to open your Hearts.

(30th May 2016)

27

LOVE AND JOY AND PEACE
EXIST EVERYWHERE

(The Circle opens with the Sounds of the Tibetan
Bowls and the Blessings Chimes)

Allow the Sound frequencies to dance a dance of Joy
through every aspect of your Being. Feel yourselves
being uplifted in every way, feeling the lightness
within your Heart as the energy of Joy rises through
your physical body to embrace your Soul Dimension,
and look out upon the world through a vista of Joy.
The Light of Joy changes your perspective of the
Earth.

You all know the phrase *'looking at the world
through rose coloured spectacles'*. This is exactly
what happens when you look out upon the world
through Joy, and you see even in the darkest parts

of your Earth there are Lights shining, Lights of Joy and happiness, and Lights of Peace, but you only see these when you look through your Heart and through your Soul, for within your Heart there is no judgment, there is total acceptance.

Love itself is non-judgmental, Joy is non-judgmental. These energies simply exist within you and it is how you work with these energies in your day to day life that creates the world around you.

Greetings Dear Hearts, I am Hilarion.

I am so blessed to join with you tonight to speak to you of Love, to speak to you of Joy, but most of all to remind you that these are your natural energies - *your natural existence is Love and Joy.* You often look outside of yourselves to find these energies, it is so much easier as Humans for you to attribute those energies to others and to believe that you need others to gift to you those energies, when in reality, Dear Hearts, you create these energies within yourself.

Look out upon your world through the eyes of Love or the eyes of Joy and you will see a totally different Earth, an Earth that is filled with potential, an earth that is filled with Blessings.

You have been told often *'like attracts like'* and you attract to yourself that which you perceive to begin with, so if you look out upon your world and see darkness and see hatred, those are the energies you will draw to yourself, for the world outside of yourself merely reflects that which you need, that which you desire, so if you look out upon your world through the eyes of Love or Joy, *'like attracts like'.* and you will begin to see the Love and the Joy that can exist, and does exist upon your Earth, and you draw those things to you, and you begin to create a whole life based upon Love and Joy.

Look around you in your life at the people you mix with, look at them with Love and Joy and you will find that those who are not of Love and Joy will disappear from your lives, for they are unable to resonate with the energies that you are sending forth.

There is so much upon your Earth that is Loving and Joyful, embrace it, feel the upliftment every day of your life, simply by looking at the world through Love and Joy.

Sometimes, Dear Hearts, Humans try too hard to create what they do not believe they already have, when they can simply *allow* everything to be in the manner they wish, and you do that simply by looking at the world with a different perspective on life. *Love and Joy and Peace exist everywhere. You seek it out by allowing it to flow firstly from you.*

That is not to say, Dear Hearts, that events can't happen in your lives that are less than Loving or Joyful, for you cannot command everyone and everything, but you can command how those things affect *You*. You can create the vibration that you wish to bring to you, so each morning as you wake and move from your bed, open your eyes with Love and Joy and then watch your day *Become* that Love and Joy.

Others will be impacted by the energies you create. Some may see and accept those energies, others may not, for they are not looking at the world through the eyes of Love and Joy, they are looking through fear and worry and concern, and they are forgetting that *'like attracts like'.*

It is your choice, your free will each day to create the world that you wish to be a part of, the world you wish to contribute to.

David J Adams

I can only invite you to look at the world through Love and Joy and help to create a whole world filled with those energies.

(26th May 2014)

28

ALLOW YOURSELVES TO GROW, AND ALLOW OTHERS TO GROW

(The Circle opens with the Sound of the Tibetan Bowls, the Drums and the Rain Stick)

Feel the shift of energy within your body as the Rain Stick cascades Love into your Heart which beats with the sound of the Drums. Allow the energy to cascade through every part of your Being, enabling you to let go the solid of the past and be uplifted by the Lightness of Love. Feel the pulsation of Light deep within your Hearts radiating forth to embrace the Earth Planet and all upon the Earth Planet with the Lightness of your Love. Allow your body to move, to shake free any last remnant of the past, the past of Duality and Separation, the past of darkness and fear, allow yourself to feel the shift of energy within you.

Greetings, Dear Hearts, I am Hilarion.

It is time for each and every one of you to become the Lightest Being that is Humanly possible. To uplift your energy into your Soul Dimension and to begin to walk a new Journey upon the Earth, a Journey in a new frequency of Light.

Throughout this past year in your time frame you have sown the seeds of the new Dimensional Frequencies into the surface and into the Centre of the New Earth, and it is time now to allow yourselves to let go of the last vestiges of the past, and to move along your path in the new Dimensional Frequencies. Feeling more powerfully than ever before the Oneness you share with all life forms upon your Planet.

You have embraced the Energies of Oneness, but you are yet to live the Energies of Oneness, but you are now ready to open your arms, to open your Hearts and embrace all around you, every Being of Light, every Being who is not yet awakened to the Light, accepting that each Being has their own path to walk - not forcing them to walk the path that you perceive, but simply being there for them when they need to ask your advice, when they need to open themselves to your Love, for Oneness is about

Sharing openly, honestly, unconditionally one with another. To let go of judgement, to embrace fully the authenticity of each Being as they present it to you.

The Old Earth Frequencies required you to want others to be in your own image, the New Earth Frequencies do not! They allow for the infinite variety that exists on your Planet, with no sense of 'better than' or 'worse than', just a simple acceptance of the variety of life that exists on the Earth that contributes fully to the beauty of the Earth. When you accept without condition all other Beings on your Planet, you will begin to find the energies of Peace and Love being harvested in every part of your World.

It is so easy to make judgements, to look at what is around you on the Earth and feel that you have failed to create what you set out to create, but that, Dear Hearts, is simply looking at your own perspectives, and not acknowledging that each other Being has their own perspective, their own journey to walk, *Honour their Journey as you would like them to Honour yours.*

There is no conflict in the variety of journeys upon your Planet - unless you choose to make that conflict!! But in the new Frequencies of Light that your Planet has absorbed in the recent past, there is less and less requirement to judge others. Allow yourselves to grow and allow others to grow, share when sharing is needed, but also be prepared to let others walk *their* journey, For without the variety of journeys upon your Planet there cannot be the perfection that you seek. For each and every Being upon the Earth is necessary for the Ascension of the Earth Planet into the Family of the Cosmos. Accept all the colours of the Earth and you will feel the Ascension within yourself – the Growth within yourself.

Let the Rain Stick speak again, that you may feel the Light and the Love and the Peace and the Joy cascading through every aspect of your Being.

(The Rain Stick is again Sounded)

LISTEN TO THE SOUND OF THE RAIN STICK. IT SPEAKS OF INFINITE VARIETY.

EMBRACE, EMBRACE, EMBRACE

(6th January 2014)

29

WE EMPOWER EACH OTHER
WITH OUR SHARING

(The Tibetan bowls, the crystal bowl and the Tingsha bells. are Sounded)

For a moment I want you to focus on the lights on the table in front of you, and embrace the colour, the many different colours, and draw these colours into your Heart, filling your Heart with Pyramids of colour, and drawing into your Hearts the Butterfly and the Dragonfly to assist you deep within for your personal transformation at the time of the shift. Recognising what you have been, and knowing deep within your Hearts that which you want to be, that which you intend to be, and call upon the Consciousness of the Butterfly and the Dragonfly to lift you from the cocoon of darkness, or from the deep well of emotions you have stored through this lifetime, that you - deep within your Hearts - may take flight and soar into the Heavens as the brightest, the most colourful Light it is possible to be.

To the Colour and Light that we have drawn into our Hearts, we now add the vibrations of Sound, for Sound and Colour are energies of upliftment. Feel the vibration of the bowls energising the Colour and the Light within your Hearts, allowing those energies to flow out from your Heart on the waves of Sound, that the Beloved Earth may hear, and see, and feel the Divine Love that is within each one of us, and that is being shared by us with Beloved Earth at this time. For we need at this time to embrace ourselves, to embrace each other, and to embrace the Earth with the most powerful frequencies of Love at our command. For it is within the Oneness of Love that the Earth will Ascend into its rightful place in the Cosmos, and *we*, as part of the Earth Consciousness, will be uplifted with the Earth.

Now take a moment and allow a space to be created within your Hearts, a space of Peace and stillness, a space of welcome for the energies of Love from Mother Earth to us - for this is not a one way flow of energy. It is a cycle of energy. We radiate it out and we receive it in, and *we empower each other with our sharing.*

Feel yourself being embraced in Oneness by *'all that is'*, upon and within the Earth, for this is a time of connection, a time of embracing the Oneness. Feel it now, in this moment, feel your connection to 'all that is'. Welcome the energies of the Earth into your Heart. Welcome the radiant energies of the Great Central Sun into your Heart, and *feel* your Heart expand and grow, and feel the powerful vibration of Love creating Peace within you - for what you create within you, is what you create around you, and the Peace and Love that is within your Hearts can be shared by all upon the Earth.

Greetings Beloved Children of Peace, I am Hilarion.

It has been my privilege for a considerable period of time to be the Guardian of the Crystal beneath the Ocean in what you call the South Pacific, that radiates forth the Blue Light, and this Crystal will play a pivotal role in attracting to it, and radiating from it, the *'Blue Mist of Peace'* that is currently making its way from the Cosmos into the outer layers of the Earth system, and ultimately into the

Earth itself. ***The 'Blue Mist of Peace' will vibrate through this Crystal out into the Oceans, and through the Oceans, to every part of the world.***

This Crystal is part of a Trinity of Crystals that is the Three Fold Flame upon the Earth, and you have worked with this Crystal for a considerable amount of time, subconsciously and occasionally consciously, but now that the Crystalline structure of the Earth has absorbed all the energies the Cosmos has sent to assist the Ascension of the Planet, the ***Three Crystals – this one radiating Blue Light, Beloved Germain's Crystal radiating Purple Light, and Beloved Djwahl Khul's Crystal radiating Gold Light - will come together as ONE, and will vibrate the frequency of Divine Love, and Divine Peace, and Divine Joy.***

So, I come to you this evening and ask you to take into your Hearts the vision of the Crystal radiating Blue Light, gifting the Love within your Hearts, and allow it to give you the ***'Blue Mist of Peace'***.

There is much being written and much being said about these special times, and your Spirit friends are all too aware of how confusing these messages may be when they come in 'overload', which is why, Dear

Hearts, we have spoken to you so much in the past few years about the need to exercise *'discernment'* at all times.

I would like you to imagine for one moment that each and every one of you are sitting atop a mountain, the same mountain, and you are looking out upon the panorama of the Earth in front of you, and you are asked to write down what you see, then - after a while - you hand what you have written to one of the number who reads out what each has seen, and you are all in awe and amazement that each and every one of you has seen something totally different.

What you are seeing of course, is all the same, but each of you will focus upon some aspect of the vista that resonates with you. *That is called discernment.* You are not overwhelmed by the vastness of the vista in front of you, because your Heart will draw you to see that which is necessary for you, that which resonates, that which is important.

So, you do not sit upon your mountain and close your eyes because the vastness of the vista is too much to bear. Instead, Dear Ones, simply look and simply accept that what you choose to see is right for you, and what others choose to see is right for them.

Now apply that, Dear Ones, to the plethora of messages that you are receiving in regards to this time upon the Earth, and know that you will choose to accept only those things which resonate with you and which are for your growth, and the rest you will let go and know that they will be relevant for others.

Do not be afraid to share what you know with others, for you cannot command them to accept what you know - *you can only place them within the consciousness, and allow each person to draw upon what is necessary for them*.

Let us all sit for a moment on top of this mountain, and look at the beauty and the vastness of beloved Planet Earth, and draw into yourself the Colour, the Light and the Sound that resonates most powerfully with you, and then simply share your joy with all those around you, those within the Human Dimension, those within the Animal Dimension, and those within the Crystal Dimension.

Being One is not being the same. Being One is simply sharing everything you are.

I embrace you with my joy, and my excitement of what is to come, and I thank you for sharing this special time with me tonight.

(3rd December 2012)

GLOSSARY

Ascended Masters - Spiritually Enlightened Beings who have previously incarnated in Human form on the Earth but who are now in Higher Dimensional Frequencies.

Shambhala - A 'City of Light' in Higher Dimensional frequencies where Spiritual and Cosmic Beings work together in Oneness. Some perceive it to be situated Energetically above the Wesak Valley in Tibet. Channeled information given to me indicates that Shambhala is a structure within the Etheric comprised of 6 energy Pyramids of the 4 sided variety, connected together to form the Sacred Geometric shape of a Merkaba.

Harmonics - A race of Universal Beings who assist Planets to hold themselves in balance through their Sound. There were originally 12 Harmonics holding the Earth in Balance, this changed in 2004 to 18 when the new 'Song of the Earth' came into being

Blessings Chimes – A hand held instrument created from wind Chimes which are used to Bless the Earth, the Oceans and all Beings of Light upon the Earth.

Crystalline Grid – A structured network of Crystals throughout the Earth that are part of the electromagnetic composition of the Earth.

Songlines – there are 12 major songlines throughout the Earth which come together at two places, Sundown Hill just outside Broken Hill in Australia (they are represented here by Sculptures) and Machu Picchu in Peru. They are vibrational, or Sound Arteries of the Planet.

Equinox - An **equinox** is commonly regarded as the moment when the plane of Earth's equator passes through the center of the Sun's disk, which occurs twice each year, around 20 March and 23 September. In other words, it is the point in which the center of the visible sun is directly over the equator.

Solstice - A **solstice** is an event occurring when the Sun appears to reach its most northerly or southerly excursion relative to the celestial_equator on the celestial sphere. Two solstices occur annually, on about 21 June and 21 December. The seasons of the year are directly connected to both the solstices and the equinoxes.

Marine Meditation – This was a Global Meditation initiated by Beloved Germain to be held at 8pm on each Equinox, wherever people were in the world. It focused on connecting with the **CONSCIOUSNESS OF THE OCEANS**. It ran from March 1991 to September 2012 - 22 years and 44 meditations in all. See http://www.dolphinempowerment.com/MarineMeditation.htm

Labyrinth: A Sacred Geometric Design or Pattern that creates a Path or journey to the center, and a return along the same route. On a Spiritual level it represents a metaphor for the journey to the centre of your deepest self, and back out into the world with a broadened understanding of who you are. With a Labyrinth there is only one choice to make, that choice is to enter or not, that choice is to walk the Spiritual path in front of you, or not. The choice is always yours to make within your Heart. There is no right or wrong way to walk a Labyrinth, you only have to enter and follow the path to the Center – the Center of yourself. Walk it in **LOVE**, walk it in **PEACE** and walk it in **RESPECT**.

Labyrinth of Divine Peace: (Front cover) The Labyrinth of Divine Peace is in the form of three Crystals coming together at their base to form a Triangle (all Cosmic creating begins with a Trinity). From the sides of this Triangle three more Crystal caves emerge, each one containing an energy necessary for the creation of Peace. These energies are the **'Twin Soul Balance'** energy, the **'Love'** energy and the **'Joy'** energy. The Labyrinth is walked in an anti clockwise direction, and the first stop is within the **'Twin Soul'** Crystal cave, then the **'Love'** Crystal cave, then the **'Joy'** Crystal cave, before you move to the centre of the Labyrinth and embrace the energies of 'Peace' represented by the Peace symbol. You move from the Centre around the outer three crystals carrying all four energies with you to share with the World. The Labyrinth of Divine Peace carries the Harmonic Note of **'Dugong'**.

SONGLINES – NAMES AND APPROXIMATE ROUTES

We have given names to the 12 Songlines that embrace the Earth Planet based on the names of the 12 Sculpture on Sundown Hill, just outside Broken Hill in New South Wales, Australia. Below we give the approximate routes that the Songlines take between Sundown Hill and Machu Picchu as they were given to us in meditation.

RAINBOW SERPENT: Sundown Hill – Willow Springs – Mount Gee (Arkaroola) – Kings Canyon (near Uluru) – Mount Kailash (Tibet) – Russia – North Pole – via the North American Spine to Machu Picchu.

MOTHERHOOD: Sundown Hill – India – South Africa – follows the Nile River to North Africa – Machu Picchu.

THE BRIDE: Sundown Hill – Pacific Rim of Fire – Machu Picchu.

MOON GODDESS: Sundown Hill – Across the Nullabor to Perth – Madagascar – Mount Kilimanjaro – Egypt (Hathor Temple) – Via the Mary Line to the United Kingdom – Machu Picchu.

BAJA EL SOL JAGUAR (UNDER THE JAGUAR SUN): Sundown Hill – Grose Valley (New South Wales) – New Zealand – Chile – Via the Spine of South America (Andes) – Machu Picchu.

ANGELS OF SUN AND MOON: Sundown Hill – Willow Springs - Curramulka (Yorke Peninsular of South Australia) – Edithburgh (also Yorke Peninsular of South Australia) - Kangaroo Island – Mount Gambier - Tasmania – South Pole - Machu Picchu.

A PRESENT TO FRED HOLLOWS IN THE AFTERLIFE: Sundown Hill – Arltunga (Central Australia) – Through the Gold Light Crystal to Brazil – along the Amazon to Machu Picchu.

TIWI TOTEMS: Sundown Hill – South Sea Islands – Hawaii – Mount Shasta (USA) – Lake

Moraine (Canada) – via Eastern Seaboard of USA to Machu Picchu.

HORSE: Sundown Hill – Philippines – China – Mongolia – Tibet – Europe – France – Machu Picchu.

FACING THE NIGHT AND DAY: Sundown Hill – Queensland (Australia) – New Guinea – Japan – North Russia to Finland – Sweden – Norway – Iceland – Tip of Greenland – Machu Picchu.

HABITAT: Sundown Hill via Inner Earth to Machu Picchu.

THOMASINA (JILARRUWI – THE IBIS): Tension Lynch pin between Sundown Hill and Machu Picchu.

HOW TO MAKE YOUR OWN BLESSINGS CHIMES

Blessings Chimes have a triangular wooden top. Inserted into the underside of the wooden triangle are a series of Screw Eyes with a series of chimes dangling from them with THREE 'Strikers' of your own design. The chimes are of different sizes, thicknesses or metals to provide a variety of Tones (which we created by taking apart a number of different, inexpensive, wind chimes). The Screw Eyes are set out in 5 rows from which the Chimes are hung, a single chime at the tip of the triangle, then 2 chimes, then 3 chimes, then 5 chimes and finally 7 chimes. This makes 18 chimes in all. One Screw Eye from which a 'Striker' hangs is placed between rows 2 and 3, and then two Screw Eyes from which 'Strikers' hang are placed between rows 4 and 5.

The 'Strikers' used in creating our Original Blessings Chime for the Marine Meditation had as decorations a Sea horse, a Unicorn, and a Dragon. The Triangular wooden top has a small knob on it, to hold as you shake the Blessings Chimes to create the vibration and resonance.

Although the original has a triangular Top and 18 chimes, you can vary this to your own intuition. The latest version that has been created for David has an Octagonal top and only 8 chimes and is called 'Peace and Harmony Chimes' rather than 'Blessings Chimes' to reflect it's more subtle Sound. Use your imagination and Intuition.

Blessings of Love and Peace

David J Adams

Printed in the United States
By Bookmasters